KitchenAid®

Cook for the Cure

Publications International, Ltd.

Pictured on the back cover: Cherry Pink Cupcakes (page 170).

ISBN: 978-1-68022-062-9

Library of Congress Control Number: 2015934782

Manufactured in China.

8 7 6 5 4 3 2 1

Since 2001, KitchenAid has proudly donated over $10 million to Susan G. Komen® through its Cook for the Cure® program including Pass the Plate, pink products, celebrity chef auctions and fundraisers hosted by supporters like you. Please visit CookfortheCure.KitchenAid.com for more information.

Komen is the world's largest breast cancer organization, funding more breast cancer research than any other nonprofit while providing real-time help to those facing the disease. Since its founding in 1982, Komen has funded more than $847 million in research and provided $1.8 billion in funding to screening, education, treatment and psychosocial support programs serving millions of people in more than 30 countries worldwide.

Komen was founded by Nancy G. Brinker, who promised her sister, Susan G. Komen, that she would end the disease that claimed Suzy's life. Visit komen.org or call 1-877 GO KOMEN. Connect with Komen on Facebook at facebook.com/susangkomen and Twitter @SusanGKomen.

In 2015, KitchenAid will donate $450,000 or more to Susan G. Komen® through the Cook for the Cure® program to support the fight against breast cancer. Product sales will not affect this donation.

Susan G. Komen's Breast Self-Awareness Messages: Know your risk; get screened; know what is normal for you; and make healthy lifestyle choices.

Contents

Introduction

In 2001, in partnership with Susan G. Komen, KitchenAid launched an initiative called Cook for the Cure to support the fight against breast cancer. The idea was simple: give those with a passion for cooking ways to contribute to the cause while engaging in their favorite pastime.

In that first year, goals for raising funds and awareness were fairly modest. Fast forward to today, and both the results and longevity of Cook for the Cure seem almost unimaginable. From widespread press coverage and adoption of the cause among celebrity chefs to the number of home cooks who have embraced the program, Cook for the Cure turned out to be both an instant and long-term success.

To date, through Cook for the Cure, $10,000,000 has been donated to Susan G. Komen to help fund important research and other vital programs.

Cook for the Cure started with donations generated through the sale of pink KitchenAid Stand Mixers, and later, other pink products. As celebrity chefs became aware of the program and wanted to participate, it grew to include auctions for culinary experiences and products signed by a "Who's Who" of the culinary world. Then came a program that encourages cooks to host their own home and office fundraisers. A "Pass the Plate" initiative was later introduced, generating donations each time special platters created by Villeroy & Boch are registered and passed from one home cook to another across the country.

Purchasing this cookbook is the latest way to show support of Cook for the Cure. Hopefully, the recipes within will inspire even more home cooks to express their passion for not just cooking, but for this important cause.

cook for the cure

Appetizers

Exotic Veggie Chips

Vegetable oil for deep frying

3 tropical tubers (malanga, yautia, lila and/or taro roots)*

1 to 2 yellow (unripe) plantains

2 parsnips, peeled

1 medium sweet potato, peeled

1 lotus root,** peeled

Coarse salt

These tubers are all similar and their labels are frequently interchangeable or overlapping. They are available in the produce sections of Latin markets. Choose whichever tubers are available and fresh. Look for firm roots without signs of mildew or soft spots.

**Lotus root is available in the produce sections of Asian markets. The outside looks like a fat beige link sausage, but has a snowflake-like pattern inside.*

1. Line two baking sheets with paper towels. Fill deep fryer or large deep saucepan with oil; heat to 350°F.

2. Peel thick shaggy skin from tubers, rinse and dry. Thinly slice tubers and place in single layers on prepared baking sheets to absorb excess moisture. (Stack in multiple layers with paper towels between layers.)

3. Peel thick skin from plantain. Slice and arrange on paper towels. Slice parsnips and sweet potato and transfer to paper towels. Trim lotus root and remove tough skin with paring knife. Slice and transfer to paper towels.

4. Working in batches, deep fry each vegetable until crisp and slightly curled, stirring occasionally. Frying time will vary from 2 to 6 minutes depending on the vegetable. Remove vegetables with slotted spoon and drain on paper towels; sprinkle with salt immediately.

5. Once drained and cooled, combine chips. Serve at once or store in airtight containers at room temperature. To recrisp chips, bake in preheated 350°F oven 5 minutes.

Makes about 6 servings

Tiny Shrimp Tacos with Peach Salsa

1 **fresh peach, peeled and finely diced**

2 **tablespoons minced red onion**

1 **jalapeño pepper, minced**

Juice of 1 lime

1 **tablespoon chopped fresh cilantro**

1 **clove garlic, minced**

½ **teaspoon salt**

8 **(6-inch) flour tortillas**

1 **tablespoon vegetable oil**

1 **pound medium raw shrimp, peeled, deveined and chopped**

2 **teaspoons chili powder**

1. Combine peach, onion, jalapeño, lime juice, cilantro, garlic and salt in medium bowl; set aside.

2. Preheat oven to 400°F. Cut out 24 rounds from tortillas with 2½-inch biscuit cutter or sharp knife. Discard scraps. Drape tortilla rounds over handle of wooden spoon; secure with toothpicks. Bake 5 minutes; repeat with remaining tortilla rounds.

3. Heat oil in large nonstick skillet over medium-high heat. Add shrimp and chili powder; sauté 3 minutes or until shrimp are pink and opaque.

4. Place shrimp in taco shells; top with peach salsa.

Makes 24 tacos

Warm Goat Cheese Rounds

2 packages (4 ounces each) goat cheese logs

2 eggs

2 tablespoons water

1 cup seasoned dry bread crumbs

4 tablespoons vegetable oil

Warm marinara sauce

1. Cut each goat cheese log crosswise into 8 rounds. (If cheese is too difficult to slice, shape scant tablespoonfuls of cheese into balls and flatten into ¼-inch-thick rounds.)

2. Beat eggs and water in small bowl. Place bread crumbs in shallow dish. Dip goat cheese rounds into egg mixture, then in bread crumbs, turning to coat all sides and gently pressing to adhere. Place on plate; freeze 10 minutes.

3. Heat 1 tablespoon oil in medium nonstick skillet over medium-high heat. Cook goat cheese rounds in batches about 2 minutes per side or until golden brown, adding additional oil as needed. Serve immediately with marinara sauce.

Makes 16 rounds

Crab-Stuffed Mushrooms

1 **pound white mushrooms (about 24), stems removed**

2 **cans (6 ounces each) lump crabmeat, drained**

½ **cup (2 ounces) shredded Monterey Jack cheese**

⅓ **cup finely chopped green onions**

3 **tablespoons mayonnaise**

2 **tablespoons shredded Parmesan cheese**

1 **tablespoon Worcestershire sauce**

1 **teaspoon minced garlic**

2 **tablespoons plain dry bread crumbs**

1. Preheat oven to 350°F. Line baking sheet with parchment paper. Place mushrooms, cap sides down, on baking sheet.

2. Combine crabmeat, Monterey Jack cheese, green onions, mayonnaise, Parmesan cheese, Worcestershire sauce and garlic in medium bowl; mix well. Spoon evenly into mushroom caps, flattening slightly, if necessary. Top evenly with bread crumbs.

3. Bake 20 minutes or until lightly browned.

Makes about 24 mushrooms

Cheesy Fondue

2 cups (8 ounces) shredded Swiss cheese

2 cups (8 ounces) shredded Monterey Jack cheese

2 tablespoons all-purpose flour

1½ cups dry white wine or apple juice

Dash ground nutmeg

Dash ground red pepper

1 loaf French bread, cut into cubes

1 Granny Smith apple, sliced

1. Combine cheeses and flour in large bowl; toss lightly to coat.

2. Bring wine to a simmer in medium saucepan over medium heat. Gradually add cheese mixture until melted, stirring constantly. Stir in nutmeg and red pepper.

3. Transfer to fondue pot; keep warm, stirring occasionally. Serve with bread cubes and apple for dipping.

Makes 4 servings

Coconut–Macadamia Shrimp

1 **pound large raw shrimp, peeled and deveined (with tails on)**

1½ **teaspoons salt, divided**

Ground red pepper

½ **cup all-purpose flour**

¼ **teaspoon freshly ground white pepper**

1 **cup flaked coconut**

⅔ **cup panko bread crumbs**

½ **cup finely chopped macadamia nuts**

2 **eggs**

¼ **cup wheat beer**

1 **cup peanut oil**

Apricot or pineapple preserves

1. Spread shrimp on paper towels and pat dry. Season with ½ teaspoon salt and red pepper.

2. Combine flour, remaining 1 teaspoon salt and white pepper in shallow dish. Combine coconut, panko and macadamia nuts in another shallow dish. Whisk eggs and beer in small bowl.

3. Heat oil in deep heavy saucepan over medium-high heat to 350°F.

4. Working in small batches, dredge shrimp in flour mixture. Dip in egg mixture and roll in coconut mixture to coat. Carefully add to oil; cook 2 minutes per side or until shrimp are pink and coating is golden. Drain on paper towels. Serve immediately with preserves for dipping.

Makes 6 to 8 servings

Goat Cheese Crostini with Sweet Onion Jam

1 tablespoon olive oil

2 medium yellow onions, thinly sliced

¾ cup dry red wine

¼ cup water

2 tablespoons packed brown sugar

1 tablespoon balsamic vinegar

1 teaspoon salt

¼ teaspoon freshly ground black pepper

2 ounces soft goat cheese

2 ounces cream cheese, softened

1 teaspoon chopped fresh thyme, plus additional for garnish

1 loaf (16 ounces) French bread, cut into 24 slices (about 1 inch thick), lightly toasted

1. Heat oil in large skillet over medium heat. Add onions; cook and stir 10 minutes. Add wine, water, brown sugar, vinegar, salt and pepper; bring to a simmer. Reduce heat to low; cook 15 to 20 minutes or until all liquid is absorbed. (If mixture appears dry, stir in additional water by tablespoons.) Cool 30 minutes or cover and refrigerate until ready to use.

2. Mix goat cheese, cream cheese and 1 teaspoon thyme in small bowl until well blended.

3. Spread ½ teaspoon goat cheese mixture on each slice of bread. Top with 1 teaspoon onion jam. Garnish with additional thyme.

Makes 24 crostini

Parmesan and Pine Nut Shortbread

- ½ **cup all-purpose flour**
- ⅓ **cup whole wheat flour**
- ⅓ **cup cornmeal**
- ¼ **teaspoon salt**
- ½ **cup (1 stick) butter, softened**
- ½ **cup shredded Parmesan cheese**
- ⅓ **cup sugar**
- ¼ **cup pine nuts**

1. Whisk flours, cornmeal and salt in small bowl.

2. Attach flat beater to stand mixer. Beat butter, cheese and sugar in mixer bowl on medium-high speed until light and fluffy. Gradually add flour mixture on low speed, mixing well after each addition. Turn out dough onto floured surface; shape into 8-inch long log 2 inches in diameter. Wrap in plastic wrap; refrigerate 30 minutes.

3. Preheat oven to 375°F. Line baking sheet with parchment paper. Cut dough into ⅓-inch slices with sharp knife. Arrange 1 inch apart on prepared baking sheet. Press 3 to 5 pine nuts onto each slice.

4. Bake 11 to 13 minutes or until firm and lightly browned. Cool on baking sheet 5 minutes. Remove to wire rack; cool completely.

Makes 26 to 28 crackers

Smoked Salmon Roses

- 1 package (8 ounces) cream cheese, softened
- 1 tablespoon prepared horseradish
- 1 tablespoon minced fresh dill
- 1 tablespoon half-and-half
- 16 slices (12 to 16 ounces) smoked salmon
- 1 red bell pepper, cut into thin strips

  Fresh dill sprigs

1. Attach flat beater to stand mixer. Beat cream cheese, horseradish, minced dill and half-and-half in mixer bowl on medium-high speed until light and creamy.

2. Spread 1 tablespoon cream cheese mixture over each salmon slice. Roll up tightly. Cut each roll in half crosswise. Arrange salmon rolls on serving dish, cut sides down, to resemble roses. Arrange pepper strip and dill sprig in center of each rose.

Makes 32 servings

Soft Pretzel Bites with Creamy Honey Mustard

¾ cup sour cream

¼ cup Dijon mustard

3 tablespoons honey

1⅔ cups warm water (110° to 115°F)

1 package (¼ ounce) active dry yeast

2 teaspoons sugar

½ teaspoon salt

4½ cups all-purpose flour, plus additional for work surface

2 tablespoons butter, softened

12 cups water

½ cup baking soda

Coarse salt

1. For creamy honey mustard, stir sour cream, mustard and honey in small bowl until smooth and well blended. Cover and refrigerate until ready to use.

2. Attach flat beater to stand mixer. Whisk 1⅔ cups warm water, yeast, sugar and table salt in mixer bowl. Let stand 5 minutes or until bubbly. Add 4½ cups flour and butter; mix on low speed until combined, scraping sides of bowl occasionally. Replace flat beater with dough hook; knead on low speed 5 to 7 minutes or until dough is smooth and elastic. Shape dough into a ball. Place dough in large lightly greased bowl; turn once to grease surface. Cover and let rise in warm place about 1 hour or until doubled.

3. Preheat oven to 450°F. Line baking sheets with foil; spray with nonstick cooking spray. Punch down dough; turn out onto floured surface. Flatten and stretch dough into 12 equal pieces. Roll each piece into 12-inch-long rope. Cut each rope into 8 equal pieces.

4. Bring 12 cups water to a boil in large saucepan. Stir in baking soda until dissolved. Working in batches, drop dough pieces into boiling water; boil 30 seconds. Remove to prepared baking sheets using slotted spoon.

5. Sprinkle dough pieces evenly with coarse salt. Bake 12 minutes or until dark golden brown, rotating baking sheets halfway through baking time. Serve with creamy honey mustard.

Makes 12 servings

Classic Tomato Bruschetta

1 tablespoon olive oil

1 clove garlic, minced

2 cups chopped seeded tomatoes (3 medium)

⅛ teaspoon salt

Freshly ground black pepper

1 loaf (16 ounces) French bread, cut into 24 slices (about 1 inch thick)

Slivered fresh basil leaves

1. Preheat oven to 350°F. Heat olive oil and garlic in small skillet over medium heat 2 minutes, stirring occasionally. Remove from heat. Stir in tomatoes, salt and pepper; mix well.

2. Place bread slices on baking sheet. Bake 8 to 10 minutes or until golden brown. Cool slightly. Top with tomato mixture and slivered basil.

Makes 24 crostini

Three-Cheese Pecan Roll

1 can (8 ounces) crushed pineapple in heavy syrup, drained

2 cups pecan pieces, toasted (see Note), divided

1 package (8 ounces) cream cheese, softened

2 cups (8 ounces) finely shredded sharp Cheddar cheese

¾ cup crumbled blue cheese

2 tablespoons Worcestershire sauce (optional)

1 teaspoon sugar

½ teaspoon red pepper flakes

Assorted crackers

1. Combine drained pineapple, 1 cup pecans, cream cheese, Cheddar cheese, blue cheese, Worcestershire sauce, if desired, sugar and red pepper flakes in large bowl.

2. Shape mixture into two balls or rolls; roll in remaining pecans to coat. Cover with plastic wrap. Freeze 30 minutes or refrigerate 2 hours or until firm. Serve with crackers.

Makes 2 cheese balls

Note: To toast pecans, spread in single layer in heavy skillet. Cook over medium heat 1 to 2 minutes or until nuts are lightly browned, stirring frequently. Remove from skillet immediately. Cool before using.

IN THE KITCHEN *with* KELLY SENYEI

Chef and author Kelly Senyei launched her blog, Just a Taste, in 2008 and has since been featured in many print publications, as well as on camera as a host, correspondent and expert in all things food and entertaining.

Overnight Cinnamon French Toast Bake

- 2 **tablespoons butter, softened**
- 5 **eggs**
- 1 **cup heavy cream**
- 1 **cup whole milk**
- 3 **tablespoons sugar**
- 1 **tablespoon vanilla**
- 2 **teaspoons ground cinnamon**
- ½ **teaspoon ground nutmeg**
- 1 **French baguette, cut into 18 (1-inch-thick) slices**
- **Maple syrup**
- **Fresh berries**

1. Grease large baking dish with butter.

2. Whisk eggs, cream, milk, sugar, vanilla, cinnamon and nutmeg in large bowl. Dip each slice of bread in egg mixture, turning to coat. Place slices in prepared baking dish, overlapping slightly. Pour any remaining egg mixture evenly over bread. Cover and refrigerate overnight.

3. Preheat oven to 375°F. Turn bread slices over. Cover baking dish tightly with foil. Bake 35 minutes or until almost set. Uncover and bake 15 to 20 minutes or until eggs are set and bread is golden brown. Serve with maple syrup and fresh berries.

Makes 6 servings

Cranberry Pomegranate Smoothies

- **1 cup frozen cranberries**
- **½ cup pomegranate juice**
- **⅓ cup plain yogurt**
- **1 banana**
- **1 tablespoon honey or agave nectar**
- **1 tablespoon ground flaxseed (optional)**

1. Combine cranberries, pomegranate juice, yogurt, banana, honey and flaxseed, if desired, in pitcher of KitchenAid® 5-Speed Diamond Blender. Blend until smooth. Taste and sweeten with additional honey, if desired.

2. Pour into two glasses; serve immediately.

Makes 2 servings

5-Minute Blueberry Coconut Frozen Yogurt

4 cups frozen blueberries

½ cup coconut-flavored yogurt

3 tablespoons honey or agave nectar

1 tablespoon fresh lemon juice

¾ cup sweetened flaked coconut, toasted* (optional)

To toast coconut, spread in shallow baking pan. Bake in preheated 350°F oven 5 to 7 minutes or until golden brown, stirring occasionally.

1. Combine blueberries, yogurt, honey and lemon juice in work bowl of KitchenAid® Pro Line® Series 16-Cup Food Processor. Process 5 minutes until smooth.

2. Serve immediately topped with toasted coconut or store in an airtight container in the freezer until ready to serve.

Makes 4 servings

Homemade Pink Beet Pasta with Garlic Brown Butter Sauce

2   **medium red beets, stemmed**

Olive oil

Salt and freshly ground black pepper

3   **eggs**

3½ **cups all-purpose flour**

½   **cup (1 stick) butter**

2   **cloves garlic, minced**

¼   **teaspoon freshly ground black pepper**

Shaved Parmesan cheese, chopped fresh chives and Himalayan pink salt (optional)

1. Preheat oven to 375°F.

2. Prick beets all over with fork. Rub lightly with olive oil; season with salt and pepper. Wrap tightly with foil; place on baking sheet. Bake 45 minutes to 1 hour or until fork-tender. Let stand until cool enough to handle.

3. Peel beets and coarsely chop. Place in small work bowl of KitchenAid® Pro Line® Series 16-Cup Food Processor. Process until smooth. Place ½ cup beet puree in medium bowl; whisk in eggs and a pinch of salt until combined.

4. Place flour in large bowl; make well in center. Place beet mixture in well; gradually stir flour into beet mixture with fork until dough begins to form. Turn out dough onto floured work surface. Knead 3 minutes or until dough is smooth, adding additional flour if dough is sticky. Wrap dough with plastic wrap; let stand at room temperature 30 minutes.

5. Sprinkle large baking sheet with flour. Cut dough into quarters. Flatten one piece of dough; dust with flour. Rewrap remaining pieces to prevent drying out. Attach KitchenAid® Pasta Roller to stand mixer and set to thickness setting 1. Turn mixer to medium speed; feed dough through rollers three or more times, folding and turning each time until smooth. If dough feels sticky, dust with flour. Change to setting 2 and feed dough sheet through rollers twice. Feed dough through once at settings 3 and 4; roll to desired thickness.

6. Let dough sheets rest on floured surface 10 minutes. Replace roller with Fettuccine Cutter. Feed dough sheets through cutter. Gather pasta into nests; place on prepared baking sheet.

7. Bring large pot of salted water to a boil. Add pasta; cook 2 to 4 minutes or until barely al dente. Drain pasta and place in large serving bowl; keep warm.

8. Place butter and garlic in medium saucepan. Cook over medium heat about 3 minutes or until butter begins to turn golden brown and foam subsides. Remove from heat; stir in ¼ teaspoon pepper. Pour over pasta; gently toss to coat. Serve with Parmesan cheese, chopped chives and pink salt, if desired.

Makes 4 to 6 servings

Brunch

Irish Porridge with Berry Compote

4 cups plus 1 tablespoon
  water, divided

½ teaspoon salt

1 cup steel-cut oats

½ teaspoon ground
  cinnamon

⅓ cup half-and-half

¼ cup packed brown sugar

1 cup fresh strawberries,
  hulled and quartered

1 container (6 ounces)
  fresh blackberries

1 container (6 ounces)
  fresh blueberries

3 tablespoons granulated
  sugar

1. Bring 4 cups water and salt to a boil in medium saucepan over medium-high heat. Whisk in oats and cinnamon. Reduce heat to medium; simmer, uncovered, about 40 minutes or until water is absorbed and oats are tender. Remove from heat; stir in half-and-half and brown sugar.

2. Meanwhile, combine strawberries, blackberries, blueberries, granulated sugar and remaining 1 tablespoon water in small saucepan; bring to a simmer over medium heat. Cook 8 to 9 minutes or until berries are tender but still hold their shape, stirring occasionally.

3. Serve porridge topped with berry compote.

Makes 4 servings

Ham and Cheese Bread Pudding

1 **small loaf (8 ounces) sourdough, country French or Italian bread, cut into 1-inch-thick slices**

3 **tablespoons butter, softened**

8 **ounces ham or smoked ham, cubed**

1 **cup (4 ounces) shredded Cheddar cheese**

3 **eggs**

2 **cups milk**

1 **teaspoon ground mustard**

½ **teaspoon salt**

⅛ **teaspoon freshly ground white pepper**

1. Grease 11×7-inch baking dish. Spread one side of each bread slice with butter. Cut into 1-inch cubes; spread in prepared baking dish. Top with ham; sprinkle with cheese.

2. Beat eggs in medium bowl. Whisk in milk, mustard, salt and pepper. Pour egg mixture evenly over bread mixture. Cover; refrigerate at least 6 hours or overnight.

3. Preheat oven to 350°F. Bake bread pudding, uncovered, 45 to 50 minutes or until puffed and golden brown and knife inserted into center comes out clean. Serve immediately.

Makes 8 servings

Fruited Granola

- **3 cups quick oats**
- **1 cup sliced almonds**
- **1 cup honey**
- **½ cup wheat germ or honey wheat germ**
- **3 tablespoons butter, melted**
- **1 teaspoon ground cinnamon**
- **3 cups whole grain cereal flakes**
- **½ cup dried blueberries or golden raisins**
- **½ cup dried cranberries or cherries**
- **½ cup dried banana chips or chopped pitted dates**

1. Preheat oven to 325°F.

2. Spread oats and almonds in single layer in 13×9-inch baking pan. Bake 15 minutes or until lightly toasted, stirring frequently.

3. Combine honey, wheat germ, butter and cinnamon in large bowl until well blended. Add oats and almonds; toss to coat completely. Spread mixture in single layer in baking pan. Bake 20 minutes or until golden brown. Cool completely in pan on wire rack. Break mixture into chunks.

4. Combine oat chunks, cereal, blueberries, cranberries and banana chips in large bowl. Store in airtight container at room temperature up to 2 weeks.

Makes about 9 cups

Blueberry–Orange French Toast Casserole

10 slices whole wheat bread, cut into 1-inch cubes

3 tablespoons butter, melted

1½ cups milk

3 eggs

½ cup sugar

1 tablespoon grated orange peel

½ teaspoon vanilla

1½ cups fresh blueberries

1. Grease 8- or 9-inch square baking dish.

2. Combine bread cubes and butter in medium bowl; toss to coat.

3. Whisk milk, eggs, sugar, orange peel and vanilla in large bowl until well blended. Add bread and blueberries; toss to coat. Pour into prepared baking dish. Cover and refrigerate at least 8 hours or overnight.

4. Preheat oven to 325°F. Bake 1 hour or until bread is browned and center is almost set. Let stand 5 minutes before serving.

Makes 6 servings

Cheese Blintzes with Blueberry-Spice Syrup

1¼ cups milk

1 cup all-purpose flour

3 eggs

1 tablespoon cornstarch

½ teaspoon salt

¼ cup (½ stick) butter, plus additional if needed, divided

½ cup fresh blueberries, divided

½ cup maple syrup, divided

½ teaspoon freshly grated lemon peel

½ teaspoon ground cinnamon

¼ teaspoon ground nutmeg

1 container (15 ounces) ricotta cheese

6 ounces cream cheese, softened

3 tablespoons sugar

¼ teaspoon almond extract

Sour cream (optional)

1. Combine milk, flour, eggs, cornstarch and salt in food processor or blender; process just until smooth. Pour into 1-quart glass measure; set aside.

2. Melt ½ teaspoon butter in medium skillet over medium heat. Pour about 3 tablespoons batter into bottom of skillet, swirling to cover bottom. Cook 1 to 2 minutes or until bottom is browned. Invert blintz onto large plate. Rub butter over browned surface.

3. Repeat step 2 with remaining batter, stacking and buttering cooked blintzes on plate.

4. For blueberry-spice syrup, bring ¼ cup blueberries and ¼ cup syrup to a boil in small saucepan over medium heat. Mash hot berries with fork. Add remaining ¼ cup blueberries, remaining ¼ cup syrup, lemon peel, cinnamon and nutmeg. Cook and stir over medium heat about 2 minutes or until heated through. Remove from heat; keep warm.

5. Attach flat beater to stand mixer. Combine ricotta cheese, cream cheese, sugar and almond extract in mixer bowl; beat on medium speed just until blended.

6. Place 2 tablespoons filling in center on unbrowned side of each blintz. Fold in sides about 1 inch; fold in opposite edges to enclose filling and form rectangular shape.

7. Melt 1 tablespoon butter in large skillet over medium heat. Cook blintzes in batches 2 minutes per side or until golden brown and heated through, adding additional butter if needed. Top with blueberry-spice syrup and sour cream, if desired.

Makes about 16 blintzes

Honey Scones with Cherry Compote

1 pound fresh Bing cherries, pitted and halved

¼ cup plus 1 tablespoon granulated sugar, divided

¼ cup water

2 tablespoons fresh lemon juice

2 cups all-purpose flour

½ cup old-fashioned oats

2 tablespoons packed brown sugar

1 tablespoon baking powder

½ teaspoon salt

6 tablespoons butter, melted

1 egg

¼ cup heavy cream

¼ cup milk

3 tablespoons honey

1. For cherry compote, combine cherries, ¼ cup granulated sugar, water and lemon juice in medium heavy saucepan. Bring to a boil over medium-high heat; boil 2 minutes. Transfer cherries to medium bowl with slotted spoon.

2. Reduce heat to medium-low; simmer liquid 2 to 4 minutes or until thickened. Return cherries to saucepan; remove from heat. Cool 1 hour before serving.

3. Preheat oven to 425°F. Line baking sheet with parchment paper.

4. Combine flour, oats, brown sugar, remaining 1 tablespoon granulated sugar, baking powder and salt in large bowl. Whisk butter, egg, cream, milk and honey in medium bowl until well blended. Add to flour mixture; stir just until dough forms. Turn out dough onto lightly floured surface. Pat into 8-inch round about ¾ inch thick. Cut into eight triangles; place 1 to 2 inches apart on prepared baking sheet.

5. Bake 12 to 15 minutes until golden brown. Cool on wire rack 15 minutes. Serve warm with cherry compote.

Makes 8 servings

Chocolate Cherry Pancakes

2 cups all-purpose flour

1 cup dried cherries

⅔ cup semisweet chocolate chips

⅓ cup sugar

4½ teaspoons baking powder

½ teaspoon baking soda

½ teaspoon salt

1½ cups milk

2 eggs

¼ cup (½ stick) butter, melted

Whipped butter and maple syrup

Note: To keep pancakes warm before serving, place a wire rack on a baking sheet and place in oven. Preheat oven to 200°F. Transfer each batch of pancakes to wire rack in single layer as they finish cooking.

1. Combine flour, dried cherries, chocolate chips, sugar, baking powder, baking soda and salt in large bowl; mix well.

2. Whisk milk, eggs and melted butter in medium bowl until well blended. Add to flour mixture; stir just until moistened.

3. Heat griddle or large nonstick skillet over medium heat until drop of water sizzles when dropped on surface. Pour batter onto griddle, ¼ cup at a time. Cook 2 to 3 minutes per side or until golden. Serve with whipped butter and maple syrup.

Makes 20 to 24 pancakes

Bacon-Cheese Grits

2 cups milk

½ cup quick-cooking grits

1½ cups (6 ounces) shredded sharp Cheddar cheese

2 tablespoons butter

1 teaspoon Worcestershire sauce

½ teaspoon salt

⅛ teaspoon ground red pepper (optional)

4 thick-cut slices bacon, crisp-cooked and chopped

1. Bring milk to a boil in large saucepan over medium-high heat. Slowly stir in grits. Return to a boil. Reduce heat; cover and simmer 5 minutes, stirring frequently.

2. Remove from heat. Stir in cheese, butter, Worcestershire sauce, salt and red pepper, if desired. Cover; let stand 2 minutes or until cheese is melted. Top each serving with bacon.

Makes 4 servings

Variation: For a thinner consistency, add an additional ½ cup milk.

French Toast Kabobs

8 slices French bread
  (about 1 inch thick)

1 cup milk

2 eggs

3 tablespoons granulated
  sugar

2 teaspoons vanilla

⅛ teaspoon salt

¾ cup fresh tangerine juice
  or orange juice

¼ cup honey

2 teaspoons cornstarch

¼ teaspoon ground ginger
  or ground cinnamon

Powdered sugar

1 container (6 ounces)
  fresh raspberries

1. Preheat broiler. Generously grease rack of broiler pan. Soak four 12-inch wooden skewers in water while preparing bread.

2. Cut bread slices in half. Beat milk, eggs, granulated sugar, vanilla and salt in shallow dish until well blended. Place bread slices in egg mixture. Let stand 5 minutes, turning to soak all sides.

3. Meanwhile, combine tangerine juice, honey, cornstarch and ginger in small saucepan; bring to a boil over medium-high heat, stirring constantly. Boil 1 minute. Reduce heat to low; keep warm.

4. Thread four pieces of bread onto each prepared skewer. Place on prepared broiler rack. Broil 4 to 5 inches from heat 5 to 7 minutes or until lightly browned. Turn skewers; broil 3 to 5 minutes or until lightly browned.

5. Spoon juice mixture onto plates; top with French toast kabobs. Sprinkle with powdered sugar and raspberries. Serve immediately.

Makes 4 servings

Raspberry Breakfast Ring

½ cup warm milk (105° to 115°F)

⅓ cup warm water (105° to 115°F)

1 package (¼ ounce) active dry yeast

3 to 3¼ cups all-purpose flour, divided

1 egg

3 tablespoons butter, melted

3 tablespoons granulated sugar

1 teaspoon salt

¼ cup raspberry fruit spread

1 teaspoon grated orange peel

⅓ cup powdered sugar

2 teaspoons fresh orange juice

Sliced almonds

1. Attach dough hook to stand mixer. Combine milk, water and yeast in mixer bowl; let stand 5 minutes.

2. Add 2¾ cups flour, egg, butter, granulated sugar and salt; mix on medium-low speed until soft dough forms. Knead about 6 minutes or until dough is smooth and elastic, adding remaining flour if necessary to prevent sticking. Place dough in large lightly greased bowl; turn once to grease surface. Cover and let rise in warm place about 45 minutes or until doubled.

3. Punch dough down. Cover and let rest in warm place 10 minutes. Line large baking sheet with parchment paper. Combine fruit spread and orange peel in small bowl; mix well.

4. Roll out dough into 16×9-inch rectangle on lightly floured surface. Spread fruit spread mixture evenly over dough. Starting with long side, tightly roll up dough; pinch seam to seal. Shape dough into ring on prepared baking sheet, keeping seam side down and pinching ends to seal.

5. Using serrated knife, cut slices three fourths of the way through dough every inch. Slightly twist each section of the dough out. Cover loosely with plastic wrap and let rise in warm place about 30 minutes or until doubled. Preheat oven to 350°F.

6. Bake about 25 minutes or until lightly browned. Remove to wire rack to cool completely.

7. Whisk powdered sugar and orange juice in small bowl until well blended. Drizzle over bread; sprinkle with almonds.

Makes 16 servings

Caramelized Bacon

12 slices (about 12 ounces) applewood-smoked bacon

½ cup packed brown sugar

2 tablespoons water

¼ to ½ teaspoon ground red pepper

1. Preheat oven to 375°F. Line 15×10-inch jelly-roll pan with heavy-duty foil. Spray wire rack with nonstick cooking spray; place in prepared pan.

2. Cut bacon in half crosswise, if desired; arrange in single layer on prepared wire rack. Combine brown sugar, water and red pepper in small bowl; mix well. Brush generously over bacon.

3. Bake 20 to 25 minutes or until bacon is well browned. Immediately remove to serving platter; cool completely.

Makes 6 servings

Note: Bacon can be prepared up to 3 days ahead and stored in the refrigerator between sheets of waxed paper in a resealable food storage bag. Let stand at room temperature at least 30 minutes before serving.

Crispy Skillet Potatoes

2 tablespoons olive oil

4 red potatoes, cut into thin wedges

½ cup chopped onion

2 tablespoons lemon pepper

½ teaspoon coarse salt

Chopped fresh parsley (optional)

1. Heat olive oil in large skillet over medium heat. Stir in potatoes, onion, lemon pepper and salt. Cover and cook 25 to 30 minutes or until potatoes are tender and browned, turning occasionally.

2. Sprinkle with parsley just before serving.

Makes 4 servings

Triple Chocolate Sticky Buns

2¾ cups bread flour

⅓ cup plus 1 tablespoon unsweetened cocoa powder, divided

¼ cup granulated sugar

1 package (¼ ounce) active dry yeast

1 teaspoon salt

½ cup sour cream

1 egg

¼ cup warm water (130°F)

10 tablespoons butter, divided

⅔ cup packed brown sugar, divided

2 tablespoons light corn syrup

½ teaspoon ground cinnamon

½ cup coarsely chopped walnuts, toasted*

½ cup semisweet chocolate chips

*To toast walnuts, spread in single layer on baking sheet. Bake in preheated 350°F oven 8 to 10 minutes or until golden brown, stirring frequently.

1. Attach flat beater to stand mixer. Whisk flour, ⅓ cup cocoa, granulated sugar, yeast and salt in mixer bowl. Whisk sour cream and egg in small bowl until well blended. Add water, 3 tablespoons butter and sour cream mixture to flour mixture; beat on medium speed 3 minutes.

2. Replace flat beater with dough hook; knead on medium-low speed about 6 minutes. Place dough in large lightly greased bowl; turn once to grease surface. Cover and let rise in warm place about 40 minutes. (Dough will not double in size.)

3. Meanwhile, prepare topping and filling. Grease 9-inch round cake pan. Combine ⅓ cup brown sugar, 4 tablespoons butter, corn syrup and remaining 1 tablespoon cocoa in small saucepan. Heat over medium heat until brown sugar dissolves and mixture bubbles around edge, stirring frequently. Pour into prepared pan.

4. Combine ⅓ cup brown sugar and cinnamon in small bowl. Melt remaining 3 tablespoons butter.

5. Roll out dough into 12×8-inch rectangle on very lightly floured surface. Brush with melted butter and sprinkle with brown sugar-cinnamon mixture. Sprinkle with walnuts and chocolate chips; gently press filling into dough. Starting with long side, roll up tightly; pinch seam to seal. Using serrated knife, cut crosswise into 12 slices; arrange over topping in pan. Cover and let rise in warm place about 35 minutes or until doubled. Preheat oven to 375°F.

6. Bake about 25 minutes or just until buns in center of pan are firm to the touch. Immediately invert onto serving plate. Serve warm or at room temperature.

Makes 12 rolls

IN THE KITCHEN *with* ALLIE ROOMBERG

Allie Roomberg is the baker and blogger behind the popular recipe site Baking a Moment, which offers unique and innovative dessert recipes for all occasions, with an emphasis on fresh, seasonal ingredients.

Coconut Lime Glazed Muffins

- 2 cups all-purpose flour
- 1 cup shredded coconut
- 1 tablespoon baking powder
- ½ teaspoon salt
  Grated peel and juice of 1 lime
- ¾ cup granulated sugar
- ¼ cup coconut oil
- 1 egg
- 1 cup coconut milk
- ½ teaspoon coconut extract
- 1 cup powdered sugar
  Lime slices (optional)

1. Preheat oven to 425°F. Spray 12 standard (2½-inch) muffin pan cups with nonstick cooking spray or line with paper baking cups. Combine flour, coconut, baking powder, salt and lime peel in small bowl.

2. Attach wire whip to KitchenAid® Stand Mixer. Place sugar and coconut oil in mixer bowl. Whip on medium speed until well blended. Add egg; whip until blended. With mixer running, add coconut milk and coconut extract until combined.

3. Replace wire whip with dough hook. Add flour mixture to sugar mixture; mix on medium speed just until blended (batter will be lumpy). *Do not overmix.* Divide batter evenly among prepared muffin cups.

4. Bake 5 minutes. *Reduce oven temperature to 350°F.* Bake 15 minutes or until toothpick inserted into centers comes out clean. Cool in pan 5 minutes. Remove to wire rack to cool completely.

5. Whisk powdered sugar and lime juice in small bowl. Dip tops of muffins in glaze; garnish with lime slices.

Makes 12 muffins

Strawberry Rose Macarons

Cookies

- **4 egg whites**
- **2 cups plus 2 tablespoons powdered sugar**
- **1¼ cups plus 2 tablespoons almond meal**
- **¼ cup plus 2 tablespoons granulated sugar**
- **Pink gel paste food coloring**

Filling

- **⅓ cup granulated sugar**
- **1 egg white**
- **6 tablespoons butter, softened**
- **3 large fresh strawberries, pureed or finely chopped**
- **5 to 6 drops rosewater**
- **2 tablespoons strawberry jam or preserves**

1. For cookies, place 4 egg whites in bowl of stand mixer. Cover and let stand until room temperature. Line two baking sheets with parchment paper.

2. Place powdered sugar and almond meal in prep bowl of KitchenAid® Pro Line® Series 16-cup Food Processor. Process until fine powder forms. Sift into medium bowl to remove any large pieces.

3. Attach wire whip and bowl to stand mixer. Whip egg whites on medium-high speed until foamy. With mixer running, gradually add ¼ cup plus 2 tablespoons granulated sugar. Tint with food coloring; whip until stiff peaks form. Fold in almond mixture with spatula until batter falls from spatula in continuous ribbon. Place batter in pastry bag fitted with large round tip. Pipe 1-inch rounds on prepared baking sheets. Rap baking sheets once against counter to remove any air bubbles. Let stand 20 to 30 minutes or until macarons do not stick when lightly touched.

4. Preheat oven to 375°F. Place one baking sheet in oven; *reduce oven temperature to 325°F.* Bake 14 minutes. Cool completely on parchment paper. Repeat with remaining baking sheet.

5. For filling, bring medium saucepan of water to a simmer. Place granulated sugar and 1 egg white in mixer bowl. Place over simmering water; cook until mixture is smooth and sugar is dissolved, whisking frequently. Attach wire whip and bowl to stand mixer. Whip egg mixture on medium-high speed until cooled completely and mixture forms stiff peaks. With mixer running, add butter 1 tablespoon at a time. If mixture appears curdled, continue to whip until it comes together before adding more butter. (If mixture is runny, refrigerate 10 to 20 minutes and whip until fluffy.) When mixture is thick and fluffy, add strawberries and rosewater; whip on high speed until fluffy and smooth. Place filling in pastry bag fitted with large round tip.

6. Pipe filling in circle on flat side of one cookie; fill with ⅛ teaspoon jam and top with another cookie.

Makes 30 macarons

Note: Macarons are best the day after they're made.

Mixed Citrus Galette

1¼ cups plus 3 tablespoons all-purpose flour, divided

¾ teaspoon kosher salt, divided

2 tablespoons olive oil

¼ cup (½ stick) cold butter, cut into thin slices

3 to 6 tablespoons ice water

7 tablespoons butter, softened

1½ cups granulated sugar, divided

1 cup finely ground walnuts

2 eggs, divided

1 tablespoon orange liqueur or vanilla

1 small grapefruit, cut into ¼-inch-thick slices

1 Meyer lemon, cut into ¼-inch-thick slices

1 Satsuma orange, cut into ¼-inch-thick slices

4 kumquats, cut into ¼-inch-thick slices

½ cup citrus juice

Sparkling sugar (optional)

1. For crust, attach wire whip to KitchenAid® stand mixer. Combine 1¼ cups flour and ½ teaspoon salt in mixer bowl. Add olive oil; mix on low speed until mixture resembles coarse meal. Add cold sliced butter; toss to coat with flour mixture. Replace wire whip with dough hook. With mixer running on low speed, drizzle in ice water until dough begins to form.

2. Turn out dough onto lightly floured surface; shape into a ball. Roll into an oval; fold into thirds. Repeat rolling and folding; wrap in plastic wrap and refrigerate 30 minutes or several days.

3. For filling, attach flat beater to stand mixer. Combine softened butter and ½ cup granulated sugar in mixer bowl; beat on medium-high speed until pale and fluffy. Add walnuts and remaining 3 tablespoons flour; mix until well blended. Add 1 egg, liqueur and remaining ¼ teaspoon salt; beat until smooth.

4. Layer grapefruit, lemon, orange and kumquat slices in medium saucepan; Add juice. Bring to a boil over medium heat. Reduce heat to low; simmer 20 minutes, swirling pan occasionally. Sprinkle with remaining 1 cup granulated sugar; simmer 20 minutes until fruit is soft and juice is syrupy, swirling pan occasionally. Remove from heat.

5. Preheat oven to 350°F. Roll out dough on lightly floured surface into ⅛-inch-thick circle. Transfer to pie plate. Spread walnut filling evenly in center of dough, leaving 3-inch border around edge. Top with fruit. Fold edge of dough over filling, pleating as needed. Beat remaining egg with 2 teaspoons water in small bowl; brush over dough and sprinkle with sparkling sugar, if desired.

6. Bake 45 minutes or until crust is golden brown. Cool slightly before slicing.

Makes 8 servings

Breads

Pull-Apart Rye Rolls

¾ cup milk

2 tablespoons butter, softened

2 tablespoons molasses

2¼ cups all-purpose flour, divided

½ cup rye flour

1 package (¼ ounce) active dry yeast

1½ teaspoons salt

1½ teaspoons caraway seeds

2 tablespoons butter, melted

1. Heat milk, softened butter and molasses in small saucepan over low heat to 120°F (butter does not need to melt completely).

2. Attach flat beater to stand mixer. Combine 1¼ cups all-purpose flour, rye flour, yeast, salt and caraway seeds in mixer bowl. Stir in milk mixture on low speed to form soft, sticky dough. Gradually add additional all-purpose flour until rough dough forms.

3. Replace flat beater with dough hook. Knead on low speed 5 to 8 minutes or until smooth and elastic, gradually adding remaining flour to prevent sticking, if necessary. Shape dough into a ball. Place dough in large lightly greased bowl; turn once to grease surface. Cover and let rise 35 to 40 minutes or until dough has increased by one third.

4. Grease 8- or 9-inch round baking pan. Turn out dough onto lightly floured surface; divide in half. Roll each half into 12-inch log. Using sharp knife, cut each log into 12 pieces; shape into tight balls. Arrange in prepared baking pan. Brush tops with melted butter. Loosely cover with lightly greased plastic wrap. Let rise in warm place about 45 minutes or until doubled.

5. Preheat oven to 375°F. Bake rolls 15 to 20 minutes or until golden brown. Cool in pan on wire rack 5 minutes. Remove to wire rack; cool completely.

Makes 24 rolls

Anadama Bread

2 cups water

½ cup yellow cornmeal

¼ cup (½ stick) butter, cut into pieces

½ cup molasses

5½ to 6 cups all-purpose flour, divided

1 package (¼ ounce) active dry yeast

1 teaspoon salt

1. Bring water to a boil in medium saucepan. Whisk in cornmeal; cook 1 minute, whisking constantly. Reduce heat to low; whisk in butter. Cook 3 minutes, stirring frequently. Stir in molasses. Transfer mixture to bowl of stand mixer; let stand 15 to 20 minutes to cool.

2. Attach flat beater to stand mixer; stir in 2 cups flour, yeast and salt on low speed until rough dough forms. Replace flat beater with dough hook. Knead on low speed 5 to 7 minutes, adding remaining flour ½ cup at a time until dough is smooth and elastic (dough will be slightly sticky). Shape dough into a ball. Place in large lightly greased bowl; turn once to grease surface. Cover and let rise in warm place about 1 hour or until doubled.

3. Punch down dough. Turn out dough onto lightly floured surface; knead 1 minute. Cut dough in half. Cover with towel; let rest 10 minutes.

4. Grease two 8-inch loaf pans. Shape dough into loaves and place in pans. Cover and let rise in warm place about 30 minutes or until doubled. Preheat oven to 350°F.

5. Bake 30 to 35 minutes or until loaves are browned and sound hollow when tapped. Immediately remove from pans; cool completely on wire racks.

Makes 2 loaves

Cinnamon-Nut Bubble Ring

¾ cup plus 1½ tablespoons milk, divided

2 tablespoons butter

3 cups bread flour, divided

¾ cup granulated sugar, divided

1 package (¼ ounce) active dry yeast

1 teaspoon salt

4½ teaspoons ground cinnamon, divided

1 egg, beaten

½ cup finely chopped walnuts

3 tablespoons butter, melted

1 cup powdered sugar

1. Heat ¾ cup milk and 2 tablespoons butter in small saucepan to 120°F (butter does not need to melt completely).

2. Attach flat beater to stand mixer. Combine 1 cup flour, ¼ cup granulated sugar, yeast, salt and ½ teaspoon cinnamon in mixer bowl. Add milk mixture and egg; mix on medium speed 3 minutes.

3. Replace flat beater with dough hook; mix in walnuts and enough remaining flour to form soft dough. Knead on low speed 5 minutes. Shape dough into a ball. Place dough in large lightly greased bowl; turn once to grease surface. Cover and let rise in warm place about 30 minutes or until doubled.

4. Grease 10-inch tube pan. Combine remaining ½ cup granulated sugar and 4 teaspoons cinnamon in shallow bowl. Place melted butter in another shallow bowl.

5. Punch down dough. Roll pieces of dough into 2-inch balls. Dip balls in melted butter; roll in cinnamon-sugar to coat. Arrange in prepared pan. Cover and let rise about 30 minutes or until doubled. Preheat oven to 350°F.

6. Bake 30 minutes or until golden brown. Cool in pan on wire rack 10 minutes; remove from pan. Combine powdered sugar and remaining 1½ tablespoons milk in small bowl; whisk until smooth. Drizzle glaze over bread.

Makes 12 servings

Cranberry–White Chocolate Scones

1 cup all-purpose flour

1 cup whole wheat flour

¼ cup plus 1 tablespoon sugar, divided

2 teaspoons baking powder

½ teaspoon salt

½ teaspoon ground nutmeg

6 tablespoons cold butter, cut into ½-inch pieces

1 cup dried cranberries

1 cup white chocolate chips

2 eggs

⅓ cup plus 1 tablespoon heavy cream, divided

Grated peel of 1 orange (3 to 4 teaspoons)

1. Preheat oven to 425°F. Line baking sheet with parchment paper.

2. Combine all-purpose flour, whole wheat flour, ¼ cup sugar, baking powder, salt and nutmeg in large bowl. Cut in butter with pastry blender until mixture resembles coarse crumbs. Stir in cranberries and white chocolate chips.

3. Beat eggs in small bowl; whisk in ⅓ cup cream and orange peel. Make well in flour mixture; add egg mixture and stir with fork just until soft dough forms.

4. Turn out dough onto lightly floured surface. Knead 8 to 10 times. Shape dough into a disc; place on prepared baking sheet and press into 9-inch circle. Score dough into eight wedges with sharp knife. Brush with remaining 1 tablespoon cream; sprinkle with remaining 1 tablespoon sugar.

5. Bake 20 to 23 minutes or until edges are lightly browned and toothpick inserted into center comes out clean. Remove to cutting board; cut into wedges along score lines. Cool slightly on wire rack; serve warm.

Makes 8 scones

Cheesy Heart Breadsticks

3 cups all-purpose flour

1 package (¼ ounce) active dry yeast

1 teaspoon salt

1 cup warm water (120°F)

¼ cup olive oil, divided

1 teaspoon dried Italian seasoning

¼ teaspoon red pepper flakes

1 cup (4 ounces) shredded Italian cheese blend

1. Attach flat beater to stand mixer. Combine flour, yeast and salt in mixer bowl. Stir in water and 2 tablespoons olive oil on low speed to form rough dough. Replace flat beater with dough hook. Knead on low speed 5 to 7 minutes or until dough is smooth and elastic. Shape dough into a ball. Place in large lightly greased bowl; turn once to grease surface. Cover and let rise in warm place 45 minutes or until doubled.

2. Preheat oven to 375°F. Line two baking sheets with parchment paper. Combine seasoning and red pepper flakes in small bowl.

3. Turn out dough onto lightly floured surface. Divide dough into eight equal pieces. Working with one piece at a time, roll dough into 14-inch rope. Shape ropes into hearts on prepared baking sheets; pinch ends together to seal. Brush hearts with remaining 2 tablespoons olive oil; sprinkle evenly with seasoning mixture. Sprinkle with cheese, pressing to adhere.

4. Bake 18 minutes or until golden brown and cheese is melted.

Makes 8 breadsticks

Honey-Fig Whole Wheat Muffins

½ cup milk

½ cup honey

¼ cup (½ stick) butter, melted

1 egg

1 cup whole wheat flour

½ cup all-purpose flour

½ cup wheat germ

2 teaspoons baking powder

1 teaspoon ground cinnamon

½ teaspoon salt

½ teaspoon ground nutmeg

1 cup chopped dried figs

½ cup chopped walnuts

1. Preheat oven to 375°F. Grease 12 standard (2½-inch) muffin cups or line with paper baking cups.

2. Combine milk, honey, butter and egg in small bowl until well blended. Combine flours, wheat germ, baking powder, cinnamon, salt and nutmeg in large bowl. Stir in milk mixture just until moistened. Fold in figs and walnuts. Spoon evenly into prepared muffin cups.

3. Bake 20 minutes or until lightly browned and toothpick inserted into centers comes out clean. Remove to wire rack to cool slightly; serve warm.

Makes 12 muffins

Blueberry Hill Bread

¾ cup buttermilk

1 egg

3 tablespoons vegetable oil or melted butter

2 cups all-purpose flour

¾ cup packed brown sugar

2 teaspoons baking powder

1 teaspoon baking soda

1 teaspoon salt

½ teaspoon ground nutmeg

1 cup fresh or frozen blueberries

1. Preheat oven to 350°F. Grease 8×4-inch loaf pan.

2. Combine buttermilk, egg and oil in small bowl. Combine flour, brown sugar, baking powder, baking soda, salt and nutmeg in large bowl. Stir in buttermilk mixture just until moistened (batter will be lumpy). *Do not overmix.* Fold in blueberries. Spread batter in prepared pan.

3. Bake 50 to 60 minutes or until toothpick inserted in center comes out clean. Cool in pan 15 minutes. Remove to wire rack to cool completely.

Makes 1 loaf

Black Forest Banana Bread

1 jar (10 ounces) maraschino cherries

1¾ cups all-purpose flour

2 teaspoons baking powder

½ teaspoon salt

⅔ cup packed brown sugar

⅓ cup butter, softened

1 cup mashed ripe bananas (about 2 large)

2 eggs

1 cup semisweet chocolate chips

¾ cup chopped pecans

1. Preheat oven to 350°F. Grease 9×5-inch loaf pan. Drain cherries, reserving 2 tablespoons juice. Coarsely chop cherries.

2. Combine flour, baking powder and salt in medium bowl.

3. Attach flat beater to stand mixer. Beat brown sugar and butter in mixer bowl on medium-high speed until creamy. Beat in bananas, eggs and reserved cherry juice until well blended. Stir in flour mixture, chopped cherries, chocolate chips and pecans on low speed just until blended. Spread batter in prepared pan.

4. Bake 1 hour or until golden brown and toothpick inserted into center comes out clean. Cool in pan 10 minutes. Remove to wire rack to cool completely.

Makes 1 loaf

IN THE KITCHEN *with* KRISTEN HESS

Kristen Hess is a Food Photographer, Food Stylist and Blogger. She is the author of TheArtfulGourmet.com, a food blog celebrating the art of food and cooking through colorful photography, recipes and stories.

Kiwi Apple Berry Blast Smoothie

1 **cup frozen blueberries**

1 **cup vanilla almond milk**

1 **package (100g) frozen unsweetened acai berry puree**

1 **apple, cored and cut into wedges**

1 **kiwi fruit, peeled**

¼ **cup raw almonds**

1 **cup vanilla Greek yogurt**

3 **tablespoons honey**

1 **tablespoon flaxseed, plus additional for garnish**

1 **teaspoon freshly grated lemon peel**

1. Place blueberries, almond milk and acai berry puree in pitcher of KitchenAid® Diamond Blender; blend on speed 1 (Stir) about 1 minute or until smooth.

2. Add apple, kiwi and almonds; blend on speed 1 (Stir) about 30 seconds. Add yogurt, honey, 1 tablespoon flaxseed and lemon peel; blend on speed 5 (Liquify) about 1 minute or until well blended. Add water to thin smoothie, if desired.

3. Pour into two glasses; garnish with additional flaxseed. Serve immediately.

Makes 2 servings

Fall Harvest Galette with Maple Sweet Potatoes, Caramelized Onions, Bacon and Gruyère

- 6 **sweet potatoes, peeled and cut into ½-inch cubes**
- 4 **tablespoons extra virgin olive oil, divided**
- 1 to 2 **tablespoons maple syrup or honey**
- 1 **tablespoon torn fresh sage leaves**

  Coarse salt and freshly ground black pepper
- 1 **large Vidalia onion, thinly sliced**
- 2 **tablespoons sugar, divided**
- ¼ **teaspoon ground nutmeg**
- 6 **slices bacon, cooked and crumbled**
- 1¼ **cups all-purpose flour**
- ¼ **teaspoon salt**
- ½ **cup (1 stick) cold butter, cut into cubes**
- 3 **tablespoons ice water**
- 1 **cup (4 ounces) shredded Gruyère cheese**
- 3 **tablespoons heavy cream or half-and-half**

  Additional torn fresh sage leaves (optional)

1. Preheat oven to 400°F. Spread sweet potatoes on large baking sheet. Drizzle with 3 tablespoons olive oil and maple syrup; sprinkle with 1 tablespoon sage season with salt and pepper. Toss until potatoes are evenly coated. Bake 25 to 30 minutes or until potatoes are tender, stirring once. Cool completely on baking sheet. *Increase oven temperature to 450°F.*

2. Heat remaining 1 tablespoon olive oil in large skillet over medium heat. Add onion and pinch of salt; cook about 20 minutes or until caramelized, stirring occasionally. Stir in 1 tablespoon sugar, nutmeg and bacon; remove from heat.

3. Attach flat beater to KitchenAid® Stand Mixer. Combine flour, remaining 1 tablespoon sugar and ¼ teaspoon salt in mixer bowl. Add butter; mix on medium-low speed until mixture resembles coarse crumbs. Add ice water 1 tablespoon at a time, mixing on low speed just until dough comes together.

4. Turn out dough onto parchment paper. Shape into a ball; flatten into a disc. Roll into 10-inch circle about ⅛-inch thick with floured rolling pin. Slide dough on parchment onto baking sheet. Spread onion mixture over dough, leaving 2-inch border; top with half of cheese and sweet potatoes. Sprinkle with remaining cheese. Fold edge of dough over filling. Brush cream over dough.

5. Bake 25 to 30 minutes or until crust is golden brown. Cool on baking sheet 10 minutes; cut into wedges to serve. Garnish with additional sage.

Makes 8 servings

King Crab BLT Sandwiches

1 pound fresh jumbo lump crabmeat

3 cups panko bread crumbs, divided

1 teaspoon Old Bay seasoning

1½ cups mayonnaise, divided

3 eggs, divided

¼ cup fresh lemon juice, divided

1 teaspoon freshly grated lemon peel

1 teaspoon Worcestershire sauce

½ teaspoon hot pepper sauce

1 jalapeño pepper *or* 2 small red chiles, seeded and finely sliced

½ cup finely diced red or yellow bell pepper

4 green onions, thinly sliced

3 tablespoons minced fresh chives, divided

¼ cup plus 2 tablespoons fresh cilantro, finely chopped, divided

1 tablespoon capers, finely chopped

1½ teaspoons sea salt, divided

1½ teaspoons freshly ground black pepper, divided

¼ cup ketchup

2 tablespoons sriracha hot sauce

2 tablespoons chile garlic sauce

1 tablespoon sesame seeds

1 tablespoon soy sauce

1 tablespoon dark sesame oil

1 cup canola oil for frying

8 ciabatta or Kaiser rolls, toasted

8 slices bacon, crisp-cooked

1 to 2 cups coleslaw

Tomato slices and baby arugula

1. Combine crab, 1½ cups panko and Old Bay seasoning in medium bowl; toss gently to mix. Whisk ½ cup mayonnaise, 1 egg, 2 tablespoons lemon juice, lemon peel, Worcestershire sauce and hot pepper sauce in large bowl until smooth. Gently fold in crab mixture until well blended. Add jalapeño, bell pepper, green onions, 2½ tablespoons chives, ¼ cup cilantro, capers, 1 teaspoon salt and 1 teaspoon black pepper; mix well. Cover and refrigerate up to 2 hours.

2. Meanwhile for spicy sesame mayonnaise, combine remaining 1 cup mayonnaise, ketchup, sriracha, chile garlic sauce, sesame seeds, soy sauce, sesame oil, remaining 2 tablespoons lemon juice, 2 tablespoons cilantro, ½ tablespoon chives, ½ teaspoon salt and ½ teaspoon black pepper. Cover and refrigerate until ready to use.

3. Whisk remaining 2 eggs in shallow bowl. Place remaining 1½ cups panko in another shallow bowl. Shape crab mixture by ⅓ cupfuls into eight 1½-inch-thick patties. Dip patties in egg mixture, then coat with panko.

4. Heat canola oil in large skillet over medium-high heat. Cook patties in batches 2 to 3 minutes per side until coating is golden brown and crisp. Drain on paper towels.

5. Serve patties on rolls with spicy sesame mayonnaise, bacon, coleslaw, tomatoes and arugula.

Makes 8 servings

Super Healthy Vegetable and Bean Soup

¼ cup extra virgin olive oil, plus additional for serving

1 large onion, chopped

3 cloves garlic, minced

½ teaspoon red pepper flakes

3 small sweet potatoes, peeled and diced

2 zucchini, diced

2 carrots, peeled and diced

2 stalks celery, diced

Coarse salt and freshly ground black pepper

8 cups chicken or vegetable broth

1 can (28 ounces) crushed Italian tomatoes

2 cans (about 15 ounces each) Great Northern beans

4 cups shredded kale

Freshly grated Parmesan cheese and grated lemon peel

1. Heat ¼ cup olive oil in Dutch oven or large saucepan over medium heat. Add onion, garlic and red pepper flakes; sauté 2 to 3 minutes or until onion is softened. Add sweet potatoes, zucchini, carrots and celery; season with salt and pepper. Sauté 5 to 7 minutes or until vegetables are softened.

2. Add broth and tomatoes; bring to a boil over medium-high heat. Reduce heat to medium; simmer 10 minutes, stirring frequently. Stir in beans and kale. Reduce heat to medium-low; simmer 15 to 20 minutes or until kale is tender.

3. Ladle soup into bowls. Top with Parmesan cheese and lemon peel; drizzle with additional olive oil, if desired.

Makes 4 to 6 servings

Lunch

Mozzarella in Carrozza

2 eggs

⅓ cup milk

¼ teaspoon salt

⅛ teaspoon freshly ground black pepper

6 ounces fresh mozzarella, cut into ¼-inch slices

8 sun-dried tomatoes packed in oil, drained and cut into strips

8 to 12 fresh basil leaves, torn

8 slices country Italian bread

1½ tablespoons olive oil

1. Whisk eggs, milk, salt and pepper in shallow bowl or baking dish until well blended.

2. Layer mozzarella, sun-dried tomatoes and basil on four slices of bread. Top with remaining bread.

3. Heat olive oil in large skillet over medium heat. Dip sandwiches in egg mixture, turning and pressing to coat completely. Add sandwiches to skillet; cook about 5 minutes per side or until golden brown. Cut into strips or squares.

Makes 4 to 8 servings

Ham and Cheese Quesadillas with Cherry Jam

2 tablespoons vegetable oil

2 cups thinly sliced red onions

2 small jalapeño peppers, seeded and minced

2 cups pitted fresh sweet cherries

2 tablespoons packed brown sugar

2 teaspoons balsamic vinegar

½ teaspoon salt

6 ounces ham, thinly sliced

4 ounces Havarti cheese, thinly sliced

4 teaspoons butter

4 (9-inch) flour tortillas

1. Heat oil in large skillet over medium-high heat. Add onion and jalapeño; sauté 3 minutes or until onions are golden. Add cherries; sauté 1 minute. Stir in brown sugar, vinegar and salt. Cook over low heat 1 minute, stirring constantly. Remove from heat; cool slightly.

2. Arrange ham slices and cheese slices over one side of each tortilla. Top with some of cherry jam. Fold tortillas in half. Set aside remaining jam.

3. Melt 2 teaspoons butter in large skillet over medium heat. Add two quesadillas; press down firmly with spatula. Cook 3 to 4 minutes per side or until golden and cheese is melted. Repeat with remaining butter and quesadillas. Cut each quesadilla in half. Serve with reserved cherry jam.

Makes 4 servings

Individual Seafood Quiche

1 **can (6 ounces) crabmeat, drained**

1 **can (4¼ ounces) salad shrimp, rinsed and drained**

1 **cup half-and-half**

2 **eggs**

2 **teaspoons seasoning blend or salt**

½ **teaspoon minced garlic**

2 **slices (2 ounces) Swiss cheese, torn into small pieces**

1. Preheat oven to 375°F. Grease four 6-ounce ramekins or jumbo (3½-inch) muffin cups.

2. Combine crabmeat, shrimp, half-and-half, eggs, seasoning blend and garlic in large bowl. Stir in cheese. Divide mixture evenly among ramekins.

3. Bake 15 to 20 minutes or until eggs are set and tops are lightly browned.

Makes 4 servings

Spanakopita Sandwiches

1 tablespoon butter

¼ cup finely chopped onion

1 clove garlic, minced

2 packages (5 ounces each) fresh baby spinach, coarsely chopped

4 ounces crumbled feta cheese

¼ teaspoon dried oregano

Pinch of ground nutmeg

4 medium croissants, split

8 slices (1 ounce each) Monterey Jack cheese

1. Melt butter in large skillet over medium heat. Add onion and garlic; sauté 5 minutes or until onion is tender. Add spinach and 1 tablespoon water; cook 5 minutes or until spinach is wilted and dry. Remove from heat; stir in feta cheese, oregano and nutmeg.

2. Divide spinach mixture evenly among croissant bottoms; top with Monterey Jack cheese and croissant tops.

3. Wipe out skillet with paper towel; heat over medium heat. Add sandwiches; cover with large lid. Cook over low heat 5 to 6 minutes or until cheese is melted and bottoms of sandwiches are golden brown.

Makes 4 sandwiches

Savory Mushroom and Brie Tart

1 cup all-purpose flour

1 teaspoon salt, divided

¼ cup (½ stick) cold butter, cut into pieces

4 tablespoons ice water

2 tablespoons butter

1 package (4 ounces) sliced exotic mushrooms (oyster, shiitake, cremini)

⅓ cup chopped shallots or sweet onion

1 tablespoon chopped fresh thyme *or* 1 teaspoon dried thyme

¼ teaspoon freshly ground black pepper

3 eggs

½ cup half-and-half or whole milk

4 ounces Brie cheese, rind removed, cut into ¼-inch cubes

1. For pastry, combine flour and ½ teaspoon salt in large bowl. Cut in cold butter with pastry blender until mixture resembles coarse crumbs. Drizzle in water 1 tablespoon at a time, tossing with fork until dough clumps together. Turn out dough onto lightly floured surface; gather dough into a ball. Wrap dough in plastic wrap; refrigerate 30 minutes.

2. Preheat oven to 350°F. Roll out dough on lightly floured surface into 12-inch circle. Fit pastry dough into 10-inch tart pan with removable bottom. Bake 10 minutes. Cool.

3. *Increase oven temperature to 375°F.* Melt 2 tablespoons butter in large skillet over medium heat. Add mushrooms and shallots; cook 5 minutes, stirring occasionally. Stir in thyme, remaining ½ teaspoon salt and pepper; cook 3 minutes or until mushroom liquid is absorbed. Remove from heat; let stand 5 minutes.

4. Whisk eggs in large bowl. Stir in half-and-half and cheese. Add mushroom mixture; mix well. Pour into prepared pie crust.

5. Bake 25 to 30 minutes or until center is set and crust is golden brown. Cool at least 10 minutes on wire cooling rack before serving. Cut into wedges; serve warm or at room temperature.

Makes 4 to 6 servings

Brie Burgers with Sun-Dried Tomato and Artichoke Spread

1 cup canned quartered artichokes, drained and chopped

½ cup sun-dried tomatoes packed in oil, drained and chopped, divided

2 tablespoons mayonnaise

1 tablespoon plus 1 teaspoon minced garlic, divided

1 teaspoon freshly ground black pepper, divided

½ teaspoon salt, divided

1½ pounds ground beef

¼ cup chopped shallots

¼ pound Brie cheese, sliced

2 tablespoons butter, softened

4 egg or Kaiser rolls, split

Heirloom tomato slices

Arugula or lettuce leaves

1. Prepare grill for direct cooking.

2. Combine artichokes, ¼ cup sun-dried tomatoes, mayonnaise, 1 teaspoon garlic, ½ teaspoon pepper and ¼ teaspoon salt in small bowl; mix well.

3. Combine beef, shallots, remaining ¼ cup sun-dried tomatoes, 1 tablespoon garlic, ½ teaspoon pepper and ¼ teaspoon salt in large bowl; mix lightly. Shape into four patties.

4. Grill over medium heat, covered, 8 to 10 minutes (or uncovered, 13 to 15 minutes) or until cooked through (160°F), turning occasionally. Top each burger with cheese during last 2 minutes of grilling.

5. Spread butter on cut surfaces of rolls; grill or toast until lightly browned. Spread artichoke mixture on bottom halves of rolls. Top with tomato slices, burger and arugula. Cover with top halves of rolls.

Makes 4 servings

Pear Gorgonzola Melts

4 ounces creamy Gorgonzola cheese (do not use crumbled blue cheese)

8 slices walnut raisin bread

2 pears, cored and sliced

½ cup fresh spinach leaves

Butter, melted

1. Spread cheese evenly on four bread slices; layer with pears and spinach. Top with remaining bread slices. Brush outsides of sandwiches with butter.

2. Heat large nonstick skillet over medium heat. Add sandwiches; cook 4 to 5 minutes per side or until cheese is melted and sandwiches are golden brown.

Makes 4 sandwiches

Havarti and Onion Sandwiches

3 teaspoons olive oil

⅔ cup thinly sliced red onion

8 slices pumpernickel bread

12 ounces dill havarti cheese, cut into slices

1 cup prepared coleslaw

1. Heat olive oil in large skillet over medium heat. Add onion; sauté 5 minutes or until tender. Layer four bread slices with onion, cheese and coleslaw; top with remaining four bread slices.

2. Heat same skillet over medium heat. Add sandwiches; press down with spatula or weigh down with small plate. Cook 4 to 5 minutes per side or until cheese is melted and sandwiches are browned.

Makes 4 sandwiches

Balsamic Onion and Prosciutto Pizzettes

3 cups all-purpose flour

1 package (¼ ounce) active dry yeast

1 teaspoon salt

1 cup warm water (120°F)

¼ cup olive oil, divided

1 large or 2 small red onions, halved and thinly sliced

¼ teaspoon salt

1½ tablespoons balsamic vinegar

⅛ teaspoon freshly ground black pepper

⅔ cup freshly grated Parmesan cheese

4 ounces fresh mozzarella, cut into small pieces

1 package (about 3 ounces) thinly sliced prosciutto, cut or torn into small pieces

1. Attach flat beater to stand mixer. Combine flour, yeast and salt in mixer bowl. Stir in water and 2 tablespoons olive oil on low speed to form rough dough. Replace flat beater with dough hook. Knead on low speed 5 to 7 minutes or until dough is smooth and elastic. Shape dough into a ball. Place in large lightly greased bowl; turn once to grease surface. Cover and let rise in warm place 45 minutes or until doubled.

2. Heat 1 tablespoon olive oil in medium skillet over medium-high heat. Add onion and salt; cook about 20 minutes or until tender and golden brown, stirring occasionally. Stir in vinegar and pepper; cook and stir 2 minutes. Set aside to cool.

3. Preheat oven to 450°F. Line two baking sheets with parchment paper.

4. Turn out dough onto lightly floured surface. Divide dough into 16 balls; press into 3-inch rounds (about ⅜ inch thick) on prepared baking sheets. Brush each round with remaining 1 tablespoon olive oil; sprinkle with about 1 teaspoon Parmesan cheese. Top with onion, mozzarella, prosciutto and remaining Parmesan cheese.

5. Bake about 13 minutes or until crusts are golden brown.

Makes 16 pizzettes

French Carrot Quiche

- 1 **pound carrots, peeled and cut into rounds**
- 1 **tablespoon butter**
- ¼ **cup chopped green onions**
- ½ **teaspoon herbes de Provence**
- 1 **cup milk**
- ¼ **cup heavy cream**
- ½ **cup all-purpose flour**
- 2 **eggs**
- ½ **teaspoon minced fresh thyme**
- ¼ **teaspoon ground nutmeg**
- ½ **cup (2 ounces) shredded Gruyère or Swiss cheese**

1. Preheat oven to 350°F. Grease four shallow 1-cup baking dishes or one 9-inch quiche dish or shallow casserole.

2. Melt butter in large skillet over medium heat. Add carrots, green onions and herbes de Provence; sauté 3 to 4 minutes or until carrots are tender.

3. Combine milk and cream in medium bowl; gradually whisk in flour. Add eggs, thyme and nutmeg; whisk until well blended. Divide carrot mixture evenly among prepared baking dishes. Top evenly with milk mixture. Sprinkle with cheese.

4. Bake 20 to 25 minutes for individual quiches or 30 to 40 minutes for 9-inch quiche or until firm. Serve warm or at room temperature.

Makes 4 servings

Grilled Prosciutto, Brie and Fig Sandwiches

½ cup fig preserves

8 slices (½ to ¾ inch thick) Italian or country bread

Freshly ground black pepper

8 to 12 ounces Brie cheese, cut into ¼-inch-thick slices

4 slices prosciutto (6-ounce package)

½ cup baby arugula

2 tablespoons butter

1. Spread preserves over four bread slices. Sprinkle pepper generously over preserves. Top with Brie, prosciutto, arugula and remaining bread slices.

2. Heat large cast iron skillet over medium heat 5 minutes. Add 1 tablespoon butter; swirl to melt and coat bottom of skillet. Add sandwiches to skillet; cook over medium-low heat about 5 minutes or until bottoms of sandwiches are golden brown.

3. Turn sandwiches and add remaining 1 tablespoon butter to skillet. Tilt pan to melt butter and move sandwiches so butter flows underneath. Cover with foil; cook about 5 minutes or until cheese is melted and bread is golden brown.

Makes 4 sandwiches

IN THE KITCHEN *with* SOMMER COLLIER

Sommer Collier is best known for her deliciously addictive food and travel blog ASpicyPerspective.com, where she shares original recipes and photography for all sort of tasty tidbits. Sommer is obsessed with creating easy-to-prepare dishes and sharing them with friends, those close and world-wide.

Steamed Root Vegetables

- 1½ **pounds mini potatoes**
- 1½ **pounds red and golden beets, peeled and quartered**
- 1 **bunch radishes, stemmed**
- 12 **cloves garlic, peeled**
- ¼ **cup chopped fresh parsley**
- 1 **tablespoon chopped fresh rosemary leaves**
- 1 **tablespoon chopped fresh sage**
- 1 **tablespoon olive oil**

  Salt and freshly ground black pepper
- ¼ **teaspoon red pepper flakes (optional)**

1. Spread potatoes, beets, radishes and garlic on large baking sheet; sprinkle with parsley, rosemary and sage and drizzle with olive oil. Season with salt and black pepper; sprinkle with red pepper flakes, if desired.

2. Place baking sheet in KitchenAid® 30-Inch Steam-Assist Double Oven and touch start. Then press Steam Cook > Auto Steam > Vegetables; the oven will set the steam temperature to 250°F for 20 minutes. Press Start and the oven will ask you to place the food in the oven, which you've already done. Press OK, and you're all set to steam.

3. Once the timer goes off, test the vegetables with a fork. If they need a few more minutes, set the oven to Manual Steam at 250°F for 5 to 7 minutes.

Makes 6 to 8 servings

Spicy Chicken and Kale Soup with Basil Cream

3½ **tablespoons olive oil, divided**

1 **red onion, chopped**

1 **fennel bulb, sliced**

2 **cloves garlic, minced**

1½ **pounds boneless skinless chicken breasts, cut into bite-size pieces**

1 **cup dry white wine**

1 **can (28 ounces) diced tomatoes**

4 **cups chicken broth**

4 **cups chopped kale**

¼ **teaspoon red pepper flakes**

1 **teaspoon salt**

½ **teaspoon freshly ground black pepper**

6 **ounces plain Greek yogurt**

1 **cup loosely packed fresh basil leaves**

1. Heat 2 tablespoons olive oil in Dutch oven or large saucepan over medium-high heat. Add onion and fennel; sauté 3 to 5 minutes or until slightly softened. Add garlic; sauté 2 to 3 minutes until vegetables are softened. Push vegetables to the side. Add chicken; sauté 3 to 5 minutes or until chicken is nearly cooked through.

2. Add wine, stirring to scrape up any browned bits from bottom of pan. Stir in tomatoes, broth, kale, red pepper flakes, 1 teaspoon salt and black pepper. Bring to a boil. Reduce heat to medium-low; simmer 20 minutes.

3. Meanwhile, combine yogurt, basil, remaining 1½ tablespoons olive oil and pinch of salt in pitcher of KitchenAid® Blender; blend until smooth. Serve soup topped with dollop of basil cream.

Makes 4 to 6 servings

Naturally Dyed Deviled Eggs

12 eggs

½ fresh beet, sliced

2 cups boiling water

6 tablespoons white vinegar, divided

½ head small red cabbage

2 cups water

½ cup mayonnaise

1 tablespoon Dijon mustard

1 teaspoon dried thyme

1 teaspoon cider vinegar

¾ teaspoon ground cumin

⅛ teaspoon ground red pepper

½ teaspoon salt

Optional toppings: crisp-cooked crumbled bacon, crispy fried shallots, capers, marinated sweet peppers, toasted pine nuts, minced fresh chives and/or rosemary

1. Place eggs in large saucepan; add cold water to cover by 1 inch. Bring to a boil over high heat; boil 12 minutes. Carefully place saucepan in sink; let stand under cold running water until cool. Add ice to water; let stand until eggs are cold, replenishing ice as needed.*

2. Meanwhile prepare the dyes. For pink dye, place beet in medium bowl. Pour boiling water and 3 tablespoons white vinegar over beet. For purple dye, combine cabbage and 2 cups water in medium saucepan; bring to a boil over medium-high heat. Remove from heat and discard cabbage when the color has been extracted. Stir in remaining 3 tablespoons white vinegar.

3. Remove eggs from ice water one at a time. Gently roll egg on hard surface to crack the shell; carefully peel egg. Cut egg in half. Place yolk in work bowl of KitchenAid® Food Processor and whites in desired dye. Repeat with remaining eggs.

4. Add mayonnaise, mustard, thyme, cider vinegar, cumin and red pepper to work bowl of food processor; process until smooth. Place mixture into piping bag fitted with desired tip.

5. Dry egg white with paper towels when desired color is reached. Pipe filling into centers and garnish with desired toppings.

Cold eggs are much easier to peel than warm eggs.

Makes 24 servings

Roasted Halibut with Microgreen Cashew Puree

4 **halibut fillets (about 1½ pounds)**

¼ **cup plus ⅓ cup grape seed oil or avocado oil, divided**

2 **tablespoons lemon juice**

1 **clove garlic, minced**

Salt and freshly ground pepper

10 **ounces microgreens, divided**

8 **fresh Thai basil leaves**

3 **tablespoons rice vinegar**

1 **tablespoon dark sesame oil**

1 **tablespoon cashew butter**

1 **tablespoon fresh grated ginger**

1 **clove garlic**

1 **teaspoon chile garlic sauce**

½ **teaspoon sea salt**

1. Preheat KitchenAid® 30-Inch Steam-Assist Double Oven to 400°F. Line large baking sheet with parchment paper. Place fish on prepared baking sheet. Whisk ¼ cup grape seed oil, lemon juice and minced garlic in small bowl; pour over fish and season with salt and pepper.

2. Bake 15 to 20 minutes or until fish is firm and flakes when tested with fork.

3. Meanwhile, combine 4 ounces microgreens, basil leaves, remaining ⅓ cup grape seed oil, vinegar, sesame oil, cashew butter, ginger, whole garlic clove, chile garlic sauce and ½ teaspoon salt in pitcher of KitchenAid® Diamond Blender. Blend until smooth.

4. Arrange remaining 6 ounces microgreens on four serving plates. Top with fish and drizzle with sauce.

Makes 4 servings

Salads

Lentil and Orzo Pasta Salad

- 8 cups water
- ½ cup dried lentils, rinsed and sorted
- 4 ounces uncooked orzo
- 1½ cups quartered cherry tomatoes
- ¾ cup finely chopped celery
- ½ cup chopped red onion
- 2 ounces pitted olives (about 16 olives), coarsely chopped
- 3 tablespoons cider vinegar
- 1 tablespoon olive oil
- 1 tablespoon dried basil
- 1 clove garlic, minced
- ⅛ teaspoon red pepper flakes
- 4 ounces feta cheese with sun-dried tomatoes and basil

1. Bring water to a boil in large saucepan over high heat. Add lentils; cook 12 minutes.

2. Add orzo; cook 10 minutes or just until tender. Drain and rinse under cold water to cool completely.

3. Combine tomatoes, celery, onion, olives, vinegar, olive oil, basil, garlic and red pepper flakes in large bowl. Add lentil mixture; toss gently to blend. Add cheese; toss gently. Let stand 15 minutes before serving.

Makes 4 servings

Marinated Tomato Salad

1½ **cups white wine vinegar or tarragon vinegar**

½ **teaspoon salt**

¼ **cup finely chopped shallots**

2 **tablespoons finely chopped chives**

2 **tablespoons fresh lemon juice**

¼ **teaspoon freshly ground white pepper**

2 **tablespoons extra virgin olive oil**

6 **plum tomatoes, quartered**

2 **large yellow tomatoes, sliced ½-inch thick**

16 **red cherry tomatoes, halved**

Sunflower sprouts (optional)

1. Combine vinegar and salt in large bowl; stir until salt is dissolved. Add shallots, chives, lemon juice and pepper; mix well. Gradually whisk in olive oil in thin steady stream until well blended.

2. Add tomatoes to marinade; toss well. Cover; let stand at room temperature 30 minutes or up to 2 hours before serving.

3. Garnish with sunflower sprouts.

Makes 8 servings

Spicy Grapefruit Salad with Raspberry Dressing

2 cups watercress

2 cups mixed salad greens

3 medium grapefruit, peeled, seeded and sectioned

½ pound jicama, peeled and cut into thin strips

1 cup fresh raspberries

2 tablespoons chopped green onion

1 tablespoon honey

1 teaspoon balsamic vinegar

½ teaspoon dry mustard

1. Combine watercress and salad greens in large bowl; divide evenly among four serving plates. Top with grapefruit and jicama.

2. Reserve 12 raspberries for garnish. Combine remaining raspberries, green onion, honey, vinegar and mustard in food processor or blender; process until smooth and well blended.

3. Drizzle dressing over salads. Top with reserved raspberries. Serve immediately.

Makes 4 servings

Mixed Greens with Pears and Goat Cheese

¼ **cup balsamic vinegar**

2 **tablespoons honey**

1½ **tablespoons olive oil**

1 **clove garlic, crushed**

½ **teaspoon salt**

¼ **teaspoon freshly ground black pepper**

1 **package (5 ounces) spring greens**

1 **cup chopped cooked chicken (about 5 ounces)**

2 **pears, thinly sliced**

½ **cup chopped celery**

⅓ **cup crumbled goat cheese**

2 **tablespoons slivered almonds**

1. Whisk vinegar, honey, olive oil, garlic, salt and pepper in small bowl until well blended.

2. Combine greens, chicken, pears, celery and goat cheese in large bowl. Drizzle dressing over salad; toss gently to coat. Top with almonds, if desired.

Makes 4 servings

Thai-Style Warm Noodle Salad

8 ounces uncooked angel hair pasta

½ cup chunky peanut butter

¼ cup soy sauce

¼ to ½ teaspoon red pepper flakes

2 green onions, thinly sliced

1 carrot, shredded

1. Cook pasta according to package directions.

2. Meanwhile, whisk peanut butter, soy sauce and red pepper flakes in serving bowl until smooth.

3. Drain pasta, reserving 5 tablespoons water. Whisk pasta water into peanut butter mixture until smooth. Add pasta; toss to coat. Stir in green onions and carrot. Serve warm or at room temperature.

Makes 4 servings

Notes: This salad can be prepared a day ahead and served warm or cold. For a heartier dish, add cubed tofu or chopped cooked chicken or beef.

Spring Greens with Blueberries and Walnuts

1 tablespoon canola oil

1 tablespoon white wine vinegar or sherry vinegar

2 teaspoons Dijon mustard

½ teaspoon salt

½ teaspoon freshly ground black pepper

1 package (5 ounces) spring greens

1 cup fresh blueberries

½ cup crumbled feta cheese

¼ cup chopped walnuts or pecans, toasted*

*To toast nuts, place in nonstick skillet. Cook and stir over medium-low heat about 5 minutes or until nuts begin to brown. Remove immediately to plate to cool.

1. Whisk oil, vinegar, mustard, salt and pepper in large bowl.

2. Add greens and blueberries; toss gently to coat. Top with cheese and walnuts. Serve immediately.

Makes 4 servings

Cobb Salad

1 package (10 ounces)
   torn mixed salad
   greens *or* 8 cups torn
   romaine lettuce

6 ounces cooked chicken
   breast, cut into
   bite-size pieces

1 tomato, seeded and
   chopped

2 hard-cooked eggs, cut
   into bite-size pieces

4 slices bacon, crisp-
   cooked and crumbled

1 ripe avocado, peeled
   and diced

1 large carrot, julienned

2 ounces crumbled blue
   cheese

   Blue cheese dressing

1. Place lettuce in serving bowl. Arrange chicken, tomato, eggs, bacon, avocado, carrot and cheese on top of lettuce.

2. Serve with dressing.

Makes 4 servings

Nectarine and Goat Cheese Salad

1 package (5 ounces)
  spring greens

2 nectarines, cut into thin
  slices

1 cup sliced celery

⅓ cup pine nuts, toasted

⅓ cup crumbled goat
  cheese

¼ cup creamy poppy seed
  dressing

1. Place greens, nectarines, celery, pine nuts and goat cheese in large bowl; toss gently to combine.

2. Drizzle dressing over salad; toss gently to coat.

Makes 4 to 6 servings

Garlic Bread and Salmon Salad

2 **slices day-old whole wheat bread**

1 **clove garlic, cut in half**

7½ **ounces canned or cooked salmon, flaked**

½ **cup chopped green onions**

1 **cup cherry or grape tomatoes, halved**

1 **teaspoon olive oil**

5 **teaspoons white wine vinegar**

1 **tablespoon tomato juice**

¼ **teaspoon salt**

¼ **teaspoon freshly ground black pepper**

2 **tablespoons minced fresh basil**

1. Preheat broiler. Position rack 3 to 4 inches from heat source. Rub one side of each bread slice with garlic. Discard garlic. Set bread, garlic side up, on broiler rack. Broil 20 to 30 seconds or until lightly browned.

2. Cut into 1-inch pieces when cool enough to handle.

3. Combine salmon, green onions and tomatoes in large serving bowl. Combine olive oil, vinegar, tomato juice, salt and pepper in small bowl. Pour over salmon mixture. Add garlic bread cubes and toss again. Sprinkle with basil.

Makes 4 servings

Fiesta Corn Salad

5 ears fresh corn

1 cup plain yogurt

3 tablespoons minced onion

1½ tablespoons fresh lime juice

1 clove garlic, minced

1 teaspoon ground cumin

1 teaspoon chili powder

¼ teaspoon salt

1½ cups shredded red cabbage

1 tomato, chopped

1 green bell pepper, seeded and chopped

5 slices bacon, crisp-cooked and crumbled

1 cup coarsely crushed tortilla chips

1 cup (4 ounces) shredded Cheddar cheese

1. Bring large pot of water to a boil. Add corn; cover and cook 6 minutes or until tender. Drain; cool completely.

2. For dressing, combine yogurt, onion, lime juice, garlic, cumin, chili powder and salt in small bowl; mix well.

3. Cut corn from cob. Combine corn, cabbage, tomato and bell pepper in large bowl. Add dressing; gently mix until well blended. Cover and refrigerate until ready to serve. Stir in bacon just before serving; sprinkle with chips and cheese.

Makes 4 to 6 servings

Rustic Dried Cherry Salad

3 cups cubed French bread

¼ cup pecans, chopped

½ cup dried sweetened cherries, chopped

1 stalk celery, diced

3 tablespoons canola oil *or* 1½ tablespoons canola oil and 1½ tablespoons olive oil

3 tablespoons raspberry vinegar

2 tablespoons water

1 tablespoon honey

¼ teaspoon curry powder

1. Preheat oven to 350°F. Spread bread cubes on baking sheet; bake 15 minutes or until toasted. Cool completely.

2. Toast pecans in medium skillet over medium heat 3 minutes or until fragrant and lightly browned, stirring frequently.

3. Combine bread, pecans, cherries and celery in large bowl.

4. Combine oil, vinegar, water, honey and curry powder in small bow; mix well. Pour over salad; toss to blend. Serve immediately.

Makes 4 servings

Bulgur, Green Bean and Orange Salad

⅔ cup bulgur

⅔ cup boiling water

1½ cups green beans, cut into 1-inch pieces

2 tablespoons olive oil

2 tablespoons lemon juice

½ teaspoon dried Greek seasoning

¼ teaspoon salt

Freshly ground black pepper

1 can (11 ounces) mandarin orange sections, drained

¼ cup slivered red onion

Spinach leaves (optional)

1. Place bulgur in medium bowl. Pour boiling water over bulgur; stir. Cover with plastic wrap; let stand 20 minutes or until bulgur is tender.

2. Bring small saucepan of water to a boil. Add green beans; cook 6 to 7 minutes or until tender; drain. For dressing, combine olive oil, lemon juice, Greek seasoning, salt and pepper to taste in small bowl; whisk until well blended.

3. Add beans, orange sections and onion to bulgur. Drizzle dressing over salad; toss gently until well blended. Cover and refrigerate at least 30 minutes. Serve on spinach leaves, if desired.

Makes 6 servings

IN THE KITCHEN *with*

TODD PORTER *and* DIANE CU

Todd Porter and Diane Cu are professional photographers and filmmakers specializing in food, travel and lifestyle and share their personal food stories and recipes on their blog, WhiteOnRiceCouple.com. Fueled by their love of storytelling, local people and culture, they document powerful food stories from around the world. They love home cooked meals made with love and are gardeners with about 40 fruit trees in their backyard.

Lavender and Honey Ice Cream

2 cups heavy cream

1 cup milk

⅓ cup honey

1 tablespoon dried lavender buds

Grated peel of 1 lemon

5 egg yolks

½ teaspoon vanilla

Pinch of coarse salt

Violet gel paste food coloring (optional)

1. Combine cream, milk, honey, lavender and lemon peel in medium saucepan. Bring to a simmer over medium heat, stirring frequently. Remove from heat. Cover and let stand 15 minutes.

2. Whisk egg yolks in medium bowl. Gradually whisk in cream mixture in thin steady stream. Pour mixture back into saucepan; stir in vanilla and salt. Cook over medium heat 4 minutes or until mixture is thick enough to coat the back of a spoon, stirring constantly. Tint with food coloring if desired (color will lighten by half while churning). Strain custard through fine-mesh sieve into medium bowl. Cover and refrigerate 3 hours or until cold.

3. Attach frozen Ice Cream Maker bowl and dasher to stand mixer. Turn mixer to stir; pour cold mixture into bowl with mixer running. Continue to stir 20 to 30 minutes or until consistency of soft serve ice cream. Transfer ice cream to airtight freezer container and freeze several hours or until frozen.

Makes 1 quart ice cream

Kung Pao Chicken Egg Rolls with Homemade Almond Butter Dipping Sauce

1 **cup whole almonds**

1 **cup cold water**

½ **cup hoisin sauce**

2 **tablespoons honey**

1 **tablespoon chile garlic sauce**

2 **teaspoons rice wine vinegar**

1 **tablespoon plus 1 teaspoon soy sauce, divided**

2 **pounds ground chicken** *or* **2 packages (16 ounces each) firm or extra firm tofu, drained and squeezed dry**

6 **green onions, finely chopped**

1 **tablespoon Chinese rice wine or dry sherry**

4 **cloves garlic, minced**

2 **teaspoons Chinese black vinegar**

2 **teaspoons oyster sauce**

½ **teaspoon sugar**

½ **teaspoon ground Szechuan pepper or freshly ground black pepper**

½ **teaspoon dark sesame oil**

12 **to 15 egg roll wrappers**

Vegetable oil or peanut oil, for frying

1. For almond butter dipping sauce, place almonds, water, hoisin sauce, honey, chile garlic sauce, rice wine vinegar and 1 teaspoon soy sauce in mini bowl of KitchenAid® 14-Cup Food Processor. Pulse on high 3 to 5 minutes or until smooth. Add additional water 1 tablespoon at a time if needed to reach desired consistency.

2. For egg rolls, combine chicken, green onions, remaining 1 tablespoon soy sauce, rice wine, garlic, black vinegar, oyster sauce, sugar, pepper and sesame oil; mix well. Let stand 20 minutes to marinate.

3. Place one egg roll wrapper on work surface with one corner facing you. Place 2 tablespoons filling on bottom end facing you. Bring bottom corner over filling and roll up gently but tightly, folding in sides and ends about halfway through rolling. Brush top corner with water; seal end. Repeat with remaining wrappers and filling.

4. Heat ¾ inch oil in large skillet over medium heat. Test heat of oil by adding a small piece of egg roll wrapper; if it sizzles and browns too quickly, the heat is too high. Carefully add egg rolls to skillet; cook 5 to 10 minutes or until golden on all sides and filling is cooked through, turning occasionally. Drain on paper towels. Serve warm with almond butter dipping sauce.

Makes 12 to 15 egg rolls

Jalapeño Cheddar Stuffed Burgers with Chipotle Guacamole

- 2 **pounds ground beef**
- 6 **ounces Cheddar cheese, sliced**
- 1 **to 2 jalapeño peppers, seeded and chopped**
  Coarse salt and freshly ground black pepper
- 3 **medium avocados, pitted and peeled**
- ¼ **cup fresh cilantro, chopped**
- 1 **teaspoon fresh lime juice**
- ½ **teaspoon ground chipotle pepper**
- ¼ **teaspoon smoked paprika**
- ½ **medium tomato, seeded and chopped**
  Vegetable oil
- 4 **to 6 hamburger buns**
  Optional toppings: greens, tomato slices, pickles and sliced jalapeño peppers

1. Prepare KitchenAid® 4 Burner Gas Grill with Side Burner for direct cooking on high heat.

2. Divide beef into four or six equal portions. Shape each portion into two flat patties. Layer half of patties with cheese, chopped jalapeños and remaining cheese. Top with remaining patties, pinching seams to seal tightly. Season patties with salt and pepper. Set aside.

3. For guacamole, mash avocados with fork to desired consistency in medium bowl. Stir in cilantro, lime juice, chipotle pepper and smoked paprika; season with salt and pepper to taste. Gently fold in chopped tomato.

4. Brush grid with vegetable oil. Place patties on grid. Grill 3 to 4 minutes per side for medium rare or to desired doneness. Grill hamburger buns until lightly toasted, if desired. Serve burgers on buns with guacamole and desired toppings.

Makes 4 to 6 servings

Grilled Rainbow Trout and Rainbow Chard with Citrus Caper Relish

1 jar (4 ounces) capers, drained

½ small red onion, minced

2 tablespoons minced fresh dill

2 tablespoons olive oil, plus additional for grilling

Grated peel of 1 lemon

1 tablespoon fresh lemon juice

1 clove garlic, minced

½ teaspoon coarse salt

Freshly ground black pepper

2 medium rainbow trout (about 1 pound each), cleaned and heads removed

2 lemons, sliced

8 to 10 sprigs fresh dill

2 medium bunches rainbow chard

1. For citrus caper relish, combine capers, onion, minced dill, 2 tablespoons olive oil, lemon peel, lemon juice, garlic and ½ teaspoon salt in medium bowl. Season with pepper to taste. Refrigerate until ready to serve.

2. Prepare KitchenAid® Grill for direct cooking on high heat.

3. Rinse trout and pat dry. Stuff cavities with lemon slices and dill sprigs. Rub outsides with olive oil and season with salt and pepper. Drizzle olive oil over chard; season with salt and pepper.

4. Carefully grease grid with oiled paper towel. Place chard on grid in single layer; grill until crisp, turning occasionally.

5. Grease grid or fish basket. Place trout on grid; grill 3 minutes per side or until golden brown and crisp.

6. Slice chard, discarding tough stems. Place chard on serving platter; top with fish. Serve warm with citrus caper relish.

Makes 2 to 4 servings

Note: Even on the best maintained grills, fish can often stick so make sure you start with a very clean grill grid. Soak paper towels with oil and use long-handled tongs to grease the hot grid just before grilling the fish. To turn fish, wait until one side is crisp and done, then gently work a spatula under it. You can also use a fish grill basket.

Entrées

Forty-Clove Chicken Filice

¼ cup olive oil

1 (3-pound) whole chicken, cut into serving pieces

40 cloves garlic (about 2 heads), peeled

½ cup dry white wine

¼ cup dry vermouth

4 stalks celery, thickly sliced

2 tablespoons finely chopped fresh parsley

2 teaspoons dried basil

1 teaspoon dried oregano

Pinch of red pepper flakes

Grated peel and juice of 1 lemon

Salt and freshly ground black pepper

1. Preheat oven to 375°F.

2. Heat olive oil in Dutch oven. Add chicken; cook until browned on all sides. Stir in garlic, wine, vermouth, celery, parsley, basil, oregano and red pepper flakes. Sprinkle lemon peel over chicken; pour lemon juice over top of chicken. Season with salt and black pepper.

3. Cover and bake 40 minutes. Remove cover; bake 15 minutes or until chicken is tender and juices run clear.

Makes 4 to 6 servings

Baked Ham with Sweet and Spicy Glaze

1 (8-pound) bone-in smoked half ham

¾ cup packed brown sugar

⅓ cup cider vinegar

¼ cup golden raisins

1 can (8¾ ounces) sliced peaches in heavy syrup, drained, chopped and syrup reserved

1 tablespoon cornstarch

¼ cup orange juice

1 can (8¼ ounces) crushed pineapple in syrup, undrained

1 tablespoon grated orange peel

1 clove garlic, minced

½ teaspoon dried red pepper flakes

½ teaspoon grated fresh ginger

1. Preheat oven to 325°F. Place ham, fat side up, in roasting pan. Bake 3 hours.

2. For glaze, combine brown sugar, vinegar, raisins and peach syrup in medium saucepan. Bring to a boil over high heat. Reduce heat to low; simmer 8 to 10 minutes.

3. Whisk cornstarch into orange juice in small bowl until smooth and well blended. Stir into brown sugar mixture. Stir pineapple, peaches, orange peel, garlic, red pepper flakes and ginger into saucepan; bring to a boil over medium heat. Cook until sauce is thickened, stirring constantly.

4. Remove ham from oven. Generously brush half of glaze over ham; bake 30 minutes or until thermometer inserted into thickest part of ham registers 160°F.

5. Remove ham from oven; brush with remaining glaze. Let stand about 20 minutes before slicing.

Makes 8 to 10 servings

Chicken Piccata

- **3 tablespoons all-purpose flour**
- **½ teaspoon salt**
- **¼ teaspoon freshly ground black pepper**
- **4 boneless skinless chicken breasts (4 ounces each)**
- **1 tablespoon olive oil**
- **1 tablespoon butter**
- **2 cloves garlic, minced**
- **¾ cup chicken broth**
- **1 tablespoon fresh lemon juice**
- **2 tablespoons chopped fresh Italian parsley**
- **1 tablespoon capers, drained**

1. Combine flour, salt and pepper in shallow bowl. Reserve 1 tablespoon flour mixture.

2. Pound chicken between waxed paper to ½-inch thickness with flat side of meat mallet or rolling pin. Coat chicken with remaining flour mixture, shaking off excess.

3. Heat olive oil and butter in large nonstick skillet over medium heat. Add chicken; cook 4 to 5 minutes per side or until no longer pink in center. Transfer to serving platter; cover loosely with foil.

4. Add garlic to same skillet; cook and stir 1 minute. Whisk in reserved flour mixture; cook and stir 1 minute. Add broth and lemon juice; cook 2 minutes or until thickened, stirring frequently. Stir in parsley and capers; spoon sauce over chicken.

Makes 4 servings

Chicken with Herb Stuffing

⅓ cup fresh basil leaves

1 package (8 ounces) goat cheese with garlic and herbs

4 boneless skinless chicken breasts (4 ounces each)

1 to 2 tablespoons olive oil

1. Preheat oven to 350°F. Place basil leaves in food processor; pulse until chopped. Cut goat cheese into large pieces and add to food processor; pulse until combined.

2. Pound chicken between waxed paper to ¼-inch thickness with flat side of meat mallet or rolling pin. Repeat with remaining chicken.

3. Shape about 2 tablespoons of cheese mixture into log and set in center of each chicken breast. Wrap chicken around filling to enclose completely. Tie securely with kitchen twine.

4. Heat 1 tablespoon olive oil in large ovenproof skillet. Add chicken bundles; cook until browned on all sides, adding additional oil as needed to prevent sticking. Bake 15 minutes or until chicken is cooked through and filling is hot. Allow to cool slightly; remove twine. Cut into slices to serve.

Makes 4 servings

Hazelnut-Coated Salmon Steaks

¼ **cup hazelnuts**

4 **salmon steaks (about 5 ounces each)**

1 **tablespoon apple butter**

1 **tablespoon Dijon mustard**

½ **teaspoon salt**

¼ **teaspoon dried thyme**

⅛ **teaspoon freshly ground black pepper**

1. Preheat oven to 375°F. Spread hazelnuts on ungreased baking sheet; bake 8 minutes or until lightly browned. Immediately transfer nuts to clean dry dish towel. Fold towel over nuts; rub vigorously to remove as much of skins as possible. Finely chop hazelnuts in food processor or with knife.

2. *Increase oven temperature to 450°F.* Place salmon in single layer in baking dish. Combine apple butter, mustard, salt, thyme and pepper in small bowl; brush over salmon. Top with hazelnuts, pressing to adhere.

3. Bake 14 to 16 minutes or until salmon begins to flake when tested with fork.

Makes 4 servings

Roasted Tomatoes, Brie and Noodles

1 **pint grape tomatoes, halved lengthwise**

2 **teaspoons canola oil**

¾ **teaspoon salt, divided**

4 **cups uncooked egg noodles**

2 **tablespoons butter**

1 **clove garlic, smashed**

2 **tablespoons all-purpose flour**

2 **cups half-and-half**

8 **ounces ripe Brie, rind removed, cut into small chunks**

2 **tablespoons minced fresh chives**

¼ **cup finely chopped fresh basil**

¼ **teaspoon freshly ground black pepper**

¼ **cup sliced almonds**

1. Preheat oven to 425°F. Line baking sheet with foil. Grease 9-inch square baking dish.

2. Spread tomatoes on prepared baking sheet. Drizzle with oil and sprinkle with ¼ teaspoon salt. Roast 20 minutes or until tender and slightly shriveled. Set aside. *Reduce oven temperature to 350°F.*

3. Meanwhile, cook noodles according to package directions. Drain and keep warm.

4. Melt butter in large saucepan or deep skillet over medium heat. Add garlic and cook 1 minute. Whisk in flour until smooth. Gradually whisk in half-and-half; cook until thickened, whisking frequently. Remove and discard garlic. Gradually stir in cheese until melted.

5. Add chives, basil, remaining ½ teaspoon salt and pepper. Stir in noodles. Drain off any liquid from tomatoes; fold into noodle mixture. Spread in prepared baking dish.

6. Bake 17 to 20 minutes or until sauce starts to bubble. Sprinkle with almonds; bake 8 to 10 minutes or until nuts are light golden brown.

Makes 6 servings

Honey-Glazed Spareribs

1 **rack pork spareribs***
   (about 2 pounds)

¼ **cup plus 1 tablespoon
   soy sauce, divided**

3 **tablespoons hoisin
   sauce**

3 **tablespoons dry sherry,
   divided**

1 **tablespoon sugar**

1 **teaspoon minced fresh
   ginger**

2 **cloves garlic, minced**

¼ **teaspoon Chinese five-
   spice powder**

2 **tablespoons honey**

1 **tablespoon cider
   vinegar**

   Sesame seeds (optional)

*Ask your butcher to cut ribs down
length of rack into two pieces so that
each half is 2 to 3 inches wide.*

1. Cut ribs into 6-inch sections. Trim excess fat. Place ribs in large resealable food storage bag.

2. For marinade, combine ¼ cup soy sauce, hoisin sauce, 2 tablespoons sherry, sugar, ginger, garlic and five-spice powder in small bowl; mix well. Pour over ribs. Seal bag; place in large bowl. Refrigerate 8 hours or overnight, turning bag occasionally.

3. Preheat oven to 350°F. Line large baking pan with foil. Place ribs on rack in pan, reserving marinade. Bake 30 minutes; turn ribs over. Brush with marinade; bake 40 minutes or until ribs are fork-tender.

4. Preheat broiler. For glaze, combine honey, vinegar, remaining 1 tablespoon soy sauce and 1 tablespoon sherry in small bowl; mix well. Brush half of mixture over ribs.

5. Broil 4 to 6 inches from heat source 2 to 3 minutes or until ribs are glazed. Turn ribs over. Brush with remaining glaze. Broil until glazed. Cut into serving-size pieces. Sprinkle with sesame seeds, if desired.

Makes about 4 servings

Pesto Lasagna

1 package (16 ounces) uncooked lasagna noodles

3 tablespoons olive oil

1½ cups chopped onions

3 cloves garlic, finely chopped

3 packages (10 ounces each) frozen chopped spinach, thawed and squeezed dry

Salt and freshly ground black pepper

3 cups (24 ounces) ricotta cheese

1½ cups pesto sauce

¾ cup grated Parmesan cheese

½ cup pine nuts, toasted*

4 cups (16 ounces) shredded mozzarella cheese

Roasted red pepper strips (optional)

*To toast pine nuts, spread in single layer in heavy skillet. Cook and stir over medium heat 1 to 2 minutes or until nuts are lightly browned, stirring frequently. Immediately remove from skillet.

1. Preheat oven to 350°F. Grease 13×9-inch casserole or lasagna pan. Partially cook lasagna noodles according to package directions.

2. Heat olive oil in large skillet over medium-high heat. Add onions and garlic; sauté until translucent. Add spinach; sauté about 5 minutes. Season with salt and black pepper. Transfer to large bowl.

3. Add ricotta cheese, pesto, Parmesan cheese and pine nuts to spinach mixture; mix well.

4. Layer five lasagna noodles, slightly overlapping, in prepared casserole. Top with one third of ricotta mixture and one third of mozzarella cheese. Repeat layers twice.

5. Bake about 35 minutes or until hot and bubbly. Garnish with red bell pepper strips.

Makes 8 servings

Rosemary–Lemon Pork Kabobs

4 red potatoes, quartered

1 pork tenderloin (about 1 pound)

1 small red onion, quartered

2 tablespoons olive oil, divided

½ teaspoon dried rosemary

Dash paprika

2 tablespoons fresh lemon juice

1 teaspoon grated lemon peel

½ clove garlic, minced

½ teaspoon salt

⅛ teaspoon freshly ground black pepper

Fresh rosemary sprigs

1. Preheat broiler. Place steamer basket in medium saucepan; add water to saucepan not touching bottom of steamer. Bring to a boil over high heat. Add potatoes; steam 6 minutes or until crisp-tender. Run under cold running water to stop cooking.

2. Cut pork into 16 (1-inch) cubes. Separate onion slices into layers.

3. Thread potatoes, pork and onion alternately onto four 10-inch metal skewers. Brush with 1 tablespoon olive oil; sprinkle with dried rosemary and paprika.

4. Place kabobs on baking sheet; broil 4 minutes. Turn; broil 4 minutes or until pork is barely pink in center.

5. Meanwhile, combine lemon juice, remaining 1 tablespoon olive oil, lemon peel, garlic, salt and pepper in small bowl. Spoon evenly over kabobs. Garnish with rosemary sprigs.

Makes 4 servings

Cornish Hens with Wild Rice and Pine Nut Pilaf

⅓ cup uncooked wild rice

4 Cornish hens (about 1¼ pounds each)

1 bunch green onions, cut into 2-inch pieces

3 tablespoons olive oil, divided

3 tablespoons soy sauce

⅓ cup pine nuts

1 cup chopped onion

1 teaspoon dried basil

2 cloves garlic, minced

2 jalapeño peppers, seeded and minced

½ teaspoon salt

Freshly ground black pepper

1. Preheat oven to 425°F. Cook rice according to package directions.

2. Stuff hens evenly with green onions; place hens on rack in roasting pan. Roast 15 minutes. Meanwhile, combine 1 tablespoon olive oil and soy sauce in small bowl. Baste hens with 1 tablespoon soy sauce mixture; roast 15 minutes or until cooked through (165°F). Baste with remaining soy sauce mixture. Let stand 15 minutes.

3. Heat large skillet over medium-high heat; add pine nuts. Cook 2 minutes or until golden, stirring constantly. Transfer to plate.

4. Add 1 tablespoon olive oil, onion and basil to same skillet; sauté 5 minutes or until golden. Add garlic; sauté 15 seconds. Remove from heat. Add rice, pine nuts, jalapeños, remaining 1 tablespoon olive oil and salt. Season with black pepper; toss gently to blend. Serve hens with rice mixture.

Makes 4 servings

IN THE KITCHEN *with* STEPHANIE WISE

Stephanie Wise is the baker and blogger behind the blog Girl Versus Dough. She writes about her adventures in bread baking and other unique, tasty recipes on her site. Her favorite things include cozy dinner parties, coffee in the morning and red wine at night, big kitchen sink salads and chocolate chip cookies straight from the oven.

Candied Bacon Maple Walnut Ice Cream

6 **egg yolks**

1¼ **cups maple syrup, divided**

1½ **cups half and half**

1 **cup heavy cream**

1 **teaspoon sea salt**

5 **slices thick-cut bacon**

½ **cup finely chopped toasted* walnuts**

*To toast nuts, place in nonstick skillet. Cook and stir over medium-low heat about 5 minutes or until nuts begin to brown. Remove immediately to plate to cool.

1. Whisk egg yolks and ¾ cup maple syrup in medium saucepan; stir in half-and-half and cream. Cook over medium heat 10 to 15 minutes until thick enough to coat the back of a spoon, whisking constantly. Remove from heat; stir in salt. Strain through fine-mesh sieve into medium bowl. Cover and refrigerate 8 hours or until cold.

2. For candied bacon, preheat oven to 400°F. Line baking sheet with foil. Place bacon in single layer on prepared baking sheet. Bake 15 minutes. Drain fat. Pour remaining ½ cup maple syrup over bacon; turn to coat with syrup. *Reduce oven temperature to 375°F.* Bake 20 minutes or until cooked through and crisp. Transfer bacon to parchment paper-lined plate; cool completely. Finely chop bacon.

3. Attach frozen Ice Cream Maker bowl and dasher to stand mixer. Turn mixer to stir; pour cold mixture into bowl with mixer running. Continue to stir 20 to 30 minutes or until consistency of soft serve ice cream. Mix in bacon and walnuts during 2 minutes of stirring. Transfer ice cream to airtight container and freeze at least 4 hours or until frozen.

Makes 6 to 8 servings

Slow Cooker Stout Short Ribs with Creamy Parmesan Polenta

3 pounds bone-in beef short ribs

Salt and freshly ground black pepper

1 tablespoon vegetable or olive oil

2 medium white onions, quartered

1 cup baby carrots

2 medium parsnips, cut into large pieces

2 to 3 medium yellow potatoes, cut into large pieces

4 sprigs *each* fresh rosemary, thyme and parsley

1 tablespoon Dijon mustard

1 tablespoon balsamic vinegar

1 bottle (12 ounces) stout

3 cups milk

1 cup water or beef broth

½ teaspoon salt

¼ teaspoon freshly ground black pepper

1 cup uncooked polenta

¼ cup freshly grated Parmesan cheese

Fresh parsley (optional)

1. Season short ribs with salt and pepper. Heat oil in large skillet over medium-high heat. Add ribs; cook 2 to 3 minutes per side or until browned.

2. Place onions and carrots in bottom of KitchenAid® 6-quart Slow Cooker; season with salt and pepper. Top with short ribs, parsnips and potatoes; add herbs, mustard and vinegar. Pour stout over all; add water just to cover.

3. Cover and cook on low 7 to 8 hours or until short ribs are cooked through and very tender and vegetables are tender. Transfer vegetables and short ribs to large bowl with slotted spoon. Strain cooking liquid; reserve for serving.

4. Meanwhile for polenta, bring milk and 1 cup water to a boil in large saucepan over medium heat. Stir in ½ teaspoon salt and ¼ teaspoon pepper; gradually stir in polenta. Cook 5 to 10 minutes or until liquid is absorbed and polenta is smooth and creamy, stirring constantly. Stir in Parmesan cheese. Serve short ribs and vegetables over polenta topped with reserved juices, if desired. Garnish with parsley.

Makes 6 to 8 servings

Pumpkin Pancakes with Cinnamon–Vanilla Syrup

1 cup water

½ cup granulated sugar

¾ cup packed brown sugar, divided

1½ cups plus 2 tablespoons all-purpose flour, divided

2 teaspoons ground cinnamon

1 teaspoon vanilla

2 teaspoons baking powder

2 teaspoons pumpkin pie spice

Pinch of salt

1½ cups milk

¾ cup solid-pack pumpkin

2 eggs

¼ cup vegetable oil

1 tablespoon butter, divided

Whipped cream and fresh berries (optional)

1. For syrup, combine water, granulated sugar, ½ cup brown sugar, 2 tablespoons flour, cinnamon and vanilla in medium saucepan. Bring to a boil over high heat, stirring constantly. Boil 3 to 5 minutes or until thickened. Remove from heat; keep warm.

2. For pancakes, combine remaining 1½ cups flour, remaining ¼ cup brown sugar, baking powder, pumpkin pie spice and salt in pitcher of blender; pulse to combine. Transfer to medium bowl.

3. Combine milk, pumpkin, eggs and oil in pitcher of blender; blend until smooth. Add flour mixture in three batches, blending well after each addition until batter is thick and smooth.

4. Heat large nonstick skillet or griddle over medium-high heat. Add 1 teaspoon butter; brush to evenly coat skillet. Drop batter into skillet by ¼ cupfuls for each pancake. Cook 2 to 3 minutes or until bubbles begin to appear on surface and edges appear dry. Turn pancakes and cook 2 to 3 minutes until golden brown. Repeat with remaining batter, adding additional butter as needed.

5. Serve pancakes warm with syrup, whipped cream and fresh berries, if desired.

Makes 10 to 12 pancakes

Roasted Summer Vegetable Soup

4 **carrots, peeled, halved and cut into 2-inch pieces**

4 **tomatoes, quartered and seeded**

2 **medium zucchini, halved and cut into 1-inch pieces**

1 **red bell pepper, seeded and sliced**

½ **yellow or white onion, sliced**

3 **cloves garlic, peeled**

1 **tablespoon fresh thyme leaves**

   Salt and freshly ground black pepper

2 **tablespoons olive oil**

2 **cups vegetable or chicken broth**

½ **teaspoon smoked paprika**

   Sour cream or crème fraîche

1. Preheat oven to 400°F. Line baking sheet with foil.

2. Spread carrots, tomatoes, zucchini, bell pepper, onion and garlic on prepared baking sheet. Sprinkle with thyme leaves and season with salt and black pepper. Drizzle with olive oil; toss to coat.

3. Bake 45 to 50 minutes or until tender and caramelized, stirring occasionally.

4. Transfer roasted vegetable mixture to pitcher of blender. Add broth and paprika; blend until smooth. Transfer soup to large saucepan; season with additional salt and pepper to taste. Cook over medium heat until heated through. Top each serving with sour cream.

Makes 4 servings

Side Dishes

Roasted Beet Risotto

2 medium beets, trimmed

4 cups vegetable broth

1 tablespoon olive oil

1 cup uncooked arborio rice

1 medium leek, finely chopped

½ cup dry white wine

½ cup crumbled goat cheese, plus additional for garnish

1 teaspoon dried Italian seasoning

¼ teaspoon salt

Juice of 1 lemon

Lemon wedges (optional)

1. Preheat oven to 400°F. Wrap each beet tightly with foil. Place on baking sheet. Roast 45 minutes to 1 hour or until knife inserted into centers goes in easily. Unwrap beets; discard foil. Let stand 15 minutes or until cool enough to handle. Peel and cut beets into bite-size pieces. Set aside.

2. Bring broth to a simmer in medium saucepan; keep warm.

3. Heat olive oil in Dutch oven or large saucepan over medium-high heat. Add rice; cook and stir 1 to 2 minutes. Add leek; cook and stir 1 to 2 minutes. Add wine; cook and stir until wine is absorbed. Add broth, ½ cup at a time, stirring constantly until broth is absorbed before adding next ½ cup. Continue adding broth and stirring until rice is tender and mixture is creamy, about 20 to 25 minutes. Remove from heat.

4. Stir in ½ cup cheese, Italian seasoning and salt. Gently stir in beets. Sprinkle with lemon juice and additional cheese, if desired. Garnish with lemon wedges. Serve immediately.

Makes 4 servings

Oven-Roasted Herbed Potatoes and Onions

3 pounds red potatoes, cut into 1½-inch cubes

1 Vidalia onion, coarsely chopped

3 tablespoons olive oil

2 tablespoons butter, melted

3 cloves garlic, minced

¾ teaspoon salt

¾ teaspoon freshly ground black pepper

⅓ cup packed chopped mixed fresh herbs, such as basil, chives, parsley, oregano, rosemary leaves, sage, tarragon and thyme

1. Preheat oven to 450°F. Line large shallow roasting pan with foil. Arrange potatoes and onion in prepared pan.

2. Combine olive oil, butter, garlic, salt and pepper in small bowl. Drizzle over vegetables; toss to coat.

3. Bake 30 minutes. Stir; bake 10 minutes. Add herbs; toss well. Bake 10 minutes or until vegetables are tender and browned.

Makes 6 servings

Mashed Carrots and Parsnips

1 medium russet potato, peeled and cut into 1-inch pieces

3 parsnips, peeled and cut into 1-inch pieces

3 carrots, cut into 1-inch pieces

1 tablespoon honey

¼ cup (½ stick) butter, softened

½ teaspoon salt

¼ teaspoon freshly ground black pepper

1. Place potato in large saucepan; add cold water to cover by 3 inches. Bring to a boil over medium-high heat; cook about 7 minutes or until potato is partially cooked.

2. Add parsnips, carrots and honey to saucepan; return to a boil. Cook 16 to 18 minutes or until vegetables are tender. Drain vegetables; return to saucepan. Add butter, salt and pepper; mash until smooth. Serve hot.

Makes 4 to 6 servings

Green Bean, Walnut and Blue Cheese Pasta Salad

2 cups uncooked gemelli pasta

2 cups trimmed halved green beans

3 tablespoons olive oil

2 tablespoons white wine vinegar

1 tablespoon chopped fresh thyme *or* 1 teaspoon dried thyme

1 tablespoon Dijon mustard

1 tablespoon fresh lemon juice

1 teaspoon honey

¼ teaspoon salt

¼ teaspoon freshly ground black pepper

½ cup chopped walnuts, toasted*

½ cup crumbled blue cheese

To toast walnuts, spread in single layer in small heavy skillet. Cook over medium heat 1 to 2 minutes until nuts are lightly browned, stirring frequently. Remove from skillet immediately. Cool before using.

1. Cook pasta according to package directions, adding green beans during last 4 minutes of cooking. Drain. Transfer to large bowl.

2. Meanwhile, whisk olive oil, vinegar, thyme, mustard, lemon juice, honey, salt and pepper in medium bowl until smooth and well blended.

3. Pour dressing over pasta and green beans; toss to coat evenly. Stir in walnuts and cheese. Serve warm or cover and refrigerate until ready to serve.**

**If serving cold, stir walnuts into salad just before serving.

Makes 8 servings

Roasted Cauliflower with Cheddar Beer Sauce

1 **large head cauliflower (about 2½ pounds), trimmed and cut into ½-inch florets**

2 **tablespoons vegetable oil, divided**

½ **teaspoon salt, divided**

½ **teaspoon freshly ground black pepper**

2 **medium shallots, finely chopped**

2 **teaspoons all-purpose flour**

½ **cup Irish ale**

1 **tablespoon spicy brown mustard**

1 **tablespoon Worcestershire sauce**

1½ **cups (6 ounces) shredded Cheddar cheese**

1. Preheat oven to 450°F. Line large baking sheet with foil.

2. Combine cauliflower, 1 tablespoon oil, ¼ teaspoon salt and pepper in medium bowl; toss to coat. Spread in single layer on prepared baking sheet.

3. Roast 25 minutes or until tender and lightly browned, stirring occasionally.

4. Meanwhile for sauce, heat remaining 1 tablespoon oil in medium saucepan over medium heat. Add shallots; sauté 3 to 4 minutes or until tender. Add flour and remaining ¼ teaspoon salt; cook and stir 1 minute. Add ale, mustard and Worcestershire sauce; bring to a simmer over medium-high heat. Reduce heat to medium-low; add cheese by ¼ cupfuls, stirring until cheese is melted before adding next addition. Cover and keep warm over low heat, stirring occasionally.

5. Transfer roasted cauliflower to large serving bowl; top with cheese sauce. Serve immediately.

Makes 4 to 6 servings

Mushroom Gratin

4 tablespoons butter, divided

1 small onion, minced

8 ounces (about 2½ cups) sliced cremini mushrooms

2 cloves garlic, minced

4 cups cooked elbow macaroni, rotini or other pasta

2 tablespoons all-purpose flour

1 cup milk

½ teaspoon salt

½ teaspoon freshly ground black pepper

½ teaspoon dry mustard

½ cup fresh bread crumbs

1 tablespoon extra virgin olive oil

1. Preheat oven to 350°F. Grease shallow baking dish or casserole.

2. Melt 2 tablespoons butter in large skillet over medium-high heat. Add onion; sauté 2 minutes. Add mushrooms and garlic; sauté 6 to 8 minutes or until softened. Remove from heat; stir in macaroni.

3. Melt remaining 2 tablespoons butter in medium saucepan over low heat. Whisk in flour; cook and stir 2 minutes without browning. Whisk in milk, salt, pepper and mustard; bring to a boil over medium-high heat, whisking constantly. Reduce heat to medium-low; cook 5 to 7 minutes or until sauce thickens, whisking constantly.

4. Pour sauce over mushroom mixture in skillet; stir to coat. Spoon into prepared baking dish. Top with bread crumbs; drizzle with olive oil.

5. Cover and bake 15 minutes. Uncover and bake 10 minutes or until bubbly and browned.

Makes 8 servings

Pasta with Caramelized Onions and Goat Cheese

1 tablespoon olive oil

6 thinly sliced sweet onions

12 ounces uncooked campanelle or orecchiette pasta

2 cloves garlic, minced

¼ cup dry white wine or vegetable broth

1 tablespoon chopped fresh sage *or* 1 teaspoon dried sage

1 teaspoon salt

¼ teaspoon freshly ground black pepper

½ cup milk

1 package (3 ounces) crumbled goat cheese

¼ cup chopped toasted walnuts

1. Heat olive oil in large skillet over medium heat. Add onions; cook 20 to 25 minutes or until golden and caramelized, stirring occasionally.

2. Meanwhile, cook pasta according to package directions. Drain and return to saucepan; keep warm.

3. Add garlic to onions in skillet; cook about 3 minutes or until softened. Add wine, sage, salt and pepper; cook until liquid has evaporated. Remove from heat. Add pasta, milk and goat cheese; stir until cheese is melted. Sprinkle with walnuts.

Makes 4 to 6 servings

Quinoa and Roasted Corn

1 cup uncooked quinoa

2 cups water

½ teaspoon salt

4 ears corn *or* 2 cups frozen corn

¼ cup plus 1 tablespoon vegetable oil, divided

1 cup chopped green onions, divided

1 teaspoon coarse salt

1 cup quartered grape tomatoes or chopped plum tomatoes, drained*

1 cup black beans, rinsed and drained

Juice of 1 lime

¼ teaspoon grated lime peel

¼ teaspoon sugar

¼ teaspoon ground cumin

¼ teaspoon freshly ground black pepper

Place tomatoes in fine-mesh strainer and place over bowl 10 to 15 minutes.

1. Place quinoa in fine-mesh strainer; rinse well under cold running water. Combine quinoa, 2 cups water and ½ teaspoon salt in medium saucepan; bring to a boil over high heat. Reduce heat to low; cover and simmer 15 to 18 minutes or until quinoa is tender and water is absorbed. Transfer to large bowl.

2. Meanwhile, remove husks and silk from corn; cut kernels off cobs. Heat ¼ cup oil in large skillet over medium-high heat. Add corn; cook 10 to 12 minutes or until tender and lightly browned, stirring occasionally. Stir in ⅔ cup green onions and coarse salt; cook and stir 2 minutes. Add corn mixture to quinoa. Gently stir in tomatoes and black beans.

3. Combine lime juice, lime peel, sugar, cumin and pepper in small bowl. Whisk in remaining 1 tablespoon oil until blended. Pour over quinoa mixture; toss lightly to coat. Sprinkle with remaining ⅓ cup green onions. Serve warm or chilled.

Makes 6 to 8 servings

Shells and Fontina

8 **ounces uncooked small pasta shells**

1¾ **cups milk**

4 **large fresh sage leaves (optional)**

¼ **cup (½ stick) butter**

¼ **cup all-purpose flour**

½ **cup tomato sauce**

Salt and freshly ground black pepper

¾ **cup freshly grated Parmesan cheese, divided**

5½ **ounces fontina cheese, shredded***

¼ **cup dry bread crumbs**

*Fontina cheese is easier to shred when very cold. Keep refrigerated or freeze 10 minutes before shredding.

1. Preheat oven to 350°F. Cook pasta according to package directions until barely al dente. Run under cold running water to stop cooking; drain.

2. Meanwhile, heat milk with sage leaves, if desired, in small saucepan over medium heat; do not boil. Melt butter in large saucepan over medium-low heat until bubbly. Whisk in flour until smooth; cook and stir 2 minutes without browning. Remove sage and gradually whisk in milk over medium heat; cook 4 to 5 minutes or until mixture begins to bubble and thickens slightly, whisking constantly. Stir in tomato sauce and season with salt and pepper. Remove from heat; stir in ½ cup Parmesan cheese until smooth.

3. Add pasta to sauce; stir to coat. Spoon one third of pasta mixture into 2-quart casserole. Top with one third of shredded fontina. Repeat layers twice. Sprinkle with bread crumbs and remaining ¼ cup Parmesan.

4. Bake 20 to 25 minutes or until hot and bubbly.

Makes 4 to 6 servings

Caramelized Brussels Sprouts with Cranberries

1 tablespoon vegetable oil

1 pound brussels sprouts, ends trimmed, thinly sliced

¼ cup dried cranberries

2 teaspoons packed brown sugar

¼ teaspoon salt

1. Heat oil in large skillet over medium-high heat. Add brussels sprouts; sauté 10 minutes or until crisp-tender and beginning to brown.

2. Add cranberries, brown sugar and salt; sauté 5 minutes or until browned.

Makes 4 servings

Fruit and Nut Quinoa

1 cup uncooked quinoa

2 cups water

1 teaspoon salt, divided

2 tablespoons finely grated orange peel, plus additional for garnish

¼ cup fresh orange juice

1 tablespoon olive oil

¼ teaspoon ground cinnamon

⅓ cup dried cranberries

⅓ cup toasted pistachio nuts*

*To toast pistachios, spread in single layer in small heavy skillet. Cook over medium heat 1 to 2 minutes or until nuts are lightly browned, stirring frequently.

1. Place quinoa in fine-mesh strainer; rinse well under cold running water. Combine quinoa, 2 cups water and ½ teaspoon salt in medium saucepan; bring to a boil over high heat. Reduce heat to low; cover and simmer 15 to 18 minutes or until quinoa is tender and water is absorbed. Stir in 2 tablespoons orange peel.

2. Whisk orange juice, olive oil, remaining ½ teaspoon salt and cinnamon in small bowl. Pour over quinoa; gently toss to coat. Fold in cranberries and pistachios. Serve warm or at room temperature. Garnish with additional orange peel.

Makes 6 servings

Tuscan Baked Rigatoni

1 package (16 ounces) uncooked rigatoni pasta

1 pound bulk Italian sausage

2 cups (8 ounces) shredded fontina cheese

2 tablespoons olive oil

2 bulbs fennel, thinly sliced

4 cloves garlic, minced

1 can (28 ounces) crushed tomatoes

1 cup heavy cream

1 teaspoon salt

1 teaspoon freshly ground black pepper

8 cups packed fresh spinach

1 can (about 15 ounces) cannellini beans, rinsed and drained

2 tablespoons pine nuts

½ cup freshly grated Parmesan cheese

1. Preheat oven to 350°F. Grease 4-quart baking dish.

2. Cook pasta according to package directions. Drain and keep warm.

3. Brown sausage in large skillet over medium-high heat, stirring to break up meat; drain fat. Transfer sausage to large bowl. Add rigatoni and fontina cheese; mix well.

4. Heat olive oil in same skillet over medium heat. Add fennel and garlic; sauté 3 minutes or until fennel is tender. Add tomatoes, cream, salt and pepper; cook until slightly thickened, stirring frequently. Stir in spinach, beans and pine nuts; cook until heated through.

5. Pour sauce mixture over pasta mixture; toss to coat. Transfer to prepared baking dish; sprinkle with Parmesan cheese. Bake 30 minutes or until bubbly and heated through.

Makes 6 to 8 servings

IN THE KITCHEN *with* LIREN BAKER

Liren Baker is the food photographer, writer and creator of the food blog Kitchen Confidante. Her appetite for all things beautiful and delicious has followed her as she lived and tasted her way throughout the country and traveled the world.

Soothing Hot Apple Berry Ginger Juice

2 apples, cored
1 cup fresh blackberries
1 cup fresh raspberries
1 slice (2 inches) fresh
   ginger

1. Assemble KitchenAid® Maximum Extraction Juicer with low pulp screen. Juice apples, berries and ginger.

2. Pour juice into small saucepan. Heat over medium heat until barely simmering. Pour into two mugs or glasses; serve immediately.

Makes 2 servings

Meyer Lemon and Raspberry Pavlovas

4 eggs, separated

2¼ cups plus 1 tablespoon sugar, divided

2 teaspoons cornstarch

1 cup plus 1 teaspoon Meyer lemon juice, divided

1 teaspoon vanilla

1 whole egg

1 pint fresh raspberries

Grated peel of 2 Meyer lemons

¼ cup (½ stick) butter, cut into cubes

3 pints fresh raspberries, divided

1 pint heavy cream

1. Preheat oven to 250°F. Line two baking sheets with parchment paper; draw two 4-inch circles on each parchment.

2. For meringue, attach wire whip to stand mixer. Place 4 egg whites in mixer bowl; whip on high speed until stiff peaks form. Gradually add 1¼ cups sugar. When egg whites appear thick and glossy, gently fold in cornstarch, 1 teaspoon lemon juice and vanilla. Spoon meringue evenly into center of circles on prepared baking sheets; spread to edges of circles, smoothing any peaks and forming wells in centers.

3. Bake about 1 hour or until meringue is light ivory and outsides are crisp. If meringue is browning or cracking, reduce oven temperature to 225°F. Turn off oven, open door slightly and let meringues cool completely in oven.

4. For lemon curd, whisk 3 egg yolks and whole egg in medium saucepan. Whisk in ¾ cup sugar, ½ cup lemon juice and lemon peel until creamy and well blended. Cook over medium heat 8 to 10 minutes or until curd is thick enough to coat the back of a spoon, whisking constantly. Remove from heat. Stir in butter one piece at a time. Strain curd through fine-mesh sieve into small bowl; press plastic wrap directly onto surface. Refrigerate 1 hour or until ready to serve.

5. For raspberry sauce, place 2 pints raspberries, remaining ½ cup lemon juice and ¼ cup sugar in pitcher of KitchenAid® Pro Line® Series 5-Speed Cordless Hand Blender. Using the star blade, puree on medium speed until the raspberries are broken down, then blend until smooth. Strain sauce through fine-mesh sieve into small bowl. Cover and refrigerate until ready to serve.

6. For whipped cream, place heavy cream and remaining 1 tablespoon sugar in clean blender pitcher. Using the whip attachment, whip the cream on high speed until cream has stiff peaks. Transfer to small bowl; cover and refrigerate until ready to serve.

7. To serve, spoon raspberry sauce onto four serving plates; top with meringues. Fill center of each meringue with ¼ cup lemon curd; top with remaining 1 pint raspberries and whipped cream. Serve immediately.

Makes 4 servings

Note: The meringues can be prepared a few days in advance. Store in a dry place in a tightly sealed container.

Tea Poached Pears with Earl Grey Ice Cream

2 cups heavy cream

1 cup whole milk

2⅔ cups granulated sugar, divided

6 Earl Grey tea bags, divided

1 vanilla bean, split and seeds scraped

Pinch of salt

4 egg yolks

4 cups water

¾ cup dried cherries

1 cinnamon stick

3 large pears, peeled, halved and cored *or* 6 small pears, peeled and kept whole

1. For ice cream, combine cream, milk, ⅓ cup sugar, 3 tea bags, vanilla pod and seeds and salt in medium saucepan. Bring to a simmer over medium heat, stirring to dissolve sugar. Remove from heat; cover and let steep 15 minutes.

2. Attach wire whip to stand mixer. Whip egg yolks in mixer bowl on medium-high speed; gradually add ⅓ cup sugar and whip until mixture is pale and thick. With mixer running, add 1 cup cream mixture in thin steady stream. Pour mixture back into saucepan. Cook over medium-low heat 5 to 8 minutes or until mixture is thick enough to coat the back of a spoon, stirring constantly. Strain mixture through fine-mesh sieve into medium bowl. Cover and refrigerate 8 hours or until cold.

3. Attach frozen Ice Cream Maker bowl and dasher to stand mixer. Turn mixer to stir; pour cold mixture into bowl with mixer running. Continue to stir 20 to 30 minutes or until consistency of soft serve ice cream. Transfer to airtight container and freeze 2 hours or until frozen.

4. For pears, bring 4 cups water to a boil in medium saucepan. Reduce heat to medium; stir in remaining 2 cups sugar, 3 tea bags, cherries and cinnamon stick. Add pears; cook 15 to 20 minutes or until tender. Transfer pears to medium bowl with slotted spoon; cool completely. Bring liquid to a boil over high heat; cook until reduced by half. Strain through fine-mesh strainer into small bowl. Cover and refrigerate until cold.

5. To serve, place pears in serving bowls; drizzle with syrup and top with ice cream.

Makes 6 servings

Raspberry, Coconut and Cardamom Panna Cotta

12 ounces fresh raspberries

¾ cup granulated sugar, divided

2 cans (14 ounces each) coconut cream

¼ cup water

1 envelope (¼ ounce) unflavored gelatin

3 cardamom pods, crushed

1. Reserve 8 to 10 raspberries for garnish; place remaining berries and ¼ cup sugar in pitcher of KitchenAid® Diamond Blender. Blend on speed 4 (Puree) until smooth. Strain through fine-mesh sieve into small bowl.

2. Combine 1 cup coconut cream and water in medium saucepan. Sprinkle gelatin over surface; let stand 5 minutes to soften. Cook and stir over low heat until gelatin dissolves. Stir in remaining coconut cream, ½ cup sugar and cardamom. Cook over medium heat until hot but not simmering, stirring occasionally. Whisk in ¼ cup raspberry puree in thin, steady stream. Remove from heat; cover and let stand 20 minutes. Strain through fine-mesh sieve into medium bowl.

3. Pour mixture into four ramekins or serving cups. Refrigerate 4 hours. Pour remaining raspberry puree over panna cotta; top with reserved raspberries.

Makes 4 servings

Desserts

Cherry Pink Cupcakes

1 jar (10 ounces) whole maraschino cherries with stems

1¼ cups all-purpose flour

1½ teaspoons baking powder

½ teaspoon salt

1 cup granulated sugar

2 eggs

½ cup vegetable oil

½ cup milk

1 teaspoon vanilla

1 cup (2 sticks) butter, softened

4 cups powdered sugar, plus additional if needed

1. Preheat oven to 350°F. Line 12 standard (2½-inch) muffin cups with paper baking cups.

2. Drain cherries reserving juice for frosting. Reserve 12 cherries for garnish; stem and chop remaining cherries and squeeze out excess moisture. Spread cherries on paper towels to drain. Set aside.

3. Combine flour, baking powder and salt in medium bowl.

4. Attach flat beater to stand mixer. Beat granulated sugar and eggs in mixer bowl on medium speed until light and fluffy. Beat in flour mixture on low speed. Add oil, milk and vanilla; beat 1 minute or until smooth. Stir in chopped cherries. Pour batter evenly into prepared muffin cups.

5. Bake 20 to 23 minutes or until lightly browned and toothpick inserted into centers comes out clean. Cool in pan on wire rack 5 minutes. Remove from pan; cool completely.

6. Meanwhile for frosting, attach flat beater to stand mixer. Beat butter in mixer bowl on medium-high speed until creamy. Add 4 cups powdered sugar; beat until blended. Add 2½ tablespoons reserved cherry juice; beat on medium-high speed until fluffy. Add additional powdered sugar if needed for desired consistency.

7. Fit piping bag with large star tip; fill with frosting. Pipe frosting in swirls on cupcakes. Garnish with reserved cherries.

Makes 12 cupcakes

Mocha Semifreddo Terrine

1½ teaspoons espresso powder

⅓ cup boiling water

2½ cups (4 ounces) amaretti cookies (about 35 cookies)

1 tablespoon unsweetened cocoa powder

3 tablespoons butter, melted

8 egg yolks

¾ cup plus 2 tablespoons sugar, divided

1 cup heavy cream

Whipped cream (optional)

1. Dissolve espresso powder in boiling water; set aside.

2. Line 9×5-inch loaf pan with plastic wrap. Place cookies and cocoa in food processor; process until cookies are finely ground. Add butter; process until well combined. Press mixture into bottom of prepared pan. Place in freezer while preparing custard.

3. Whisk egg yolks and ¾ cup sugar in top of double boiler or medium metal bowl. Stir in cooled espresso mixture. Place over simmering water. Cook 4 to 5 minutes or until mixture thickens, whisking constantly. Remove from heat; place bowl in pan of ice water. Whisk mixture 1 minute. Let stand in ice water 5 minutes or until cooled to room temperature, whisking occasionally.

4. Attach wire whip to stand mixer. Whip cream and remaining 2 tablespoons sugar in mixer bowl on high speed until stiff peaks form. Gently fold whipped cream into cooled custard. Spread mixture over crust in pan. Cover tightly; freeze until firm, at least 8 hours or up to 24 hours before serving.

5. To serve, invert terrine onto serving plate; remove plastic wrap. Cut into slices. Serve on chilled plates topped with whipped cream, if desired.

Makes 8 to 12 servings

Strawberry Rhubarb Pie

2½ cups all-purpose flour

1 teaspoon salt

1½ cups plus 1 teaspoon sugar, divided

1 cup (2 sticks) cold butter, cubed

7 tablespoons ice water

1 tablespoon cider vinegar

½ cup cornstarch

2 tablespoons quick-cooking tapioca

1 tablespoon grated lemon peel

¼ teaspoon ground allspice

4 cups sliced rhubarb (1-inch pieces)

3 cups sliced fresh strawberries

1 egg, lightly beaten

1. Attach flat beater to stand mixer. Combine flour, salt and 1 teaspoon sugar in mixer bowl. Add butter; mix on low speed 1 minute or until coarse crumbs form.

2. Combine ice water and vinegar in small bowl. With mixer running on low speed, drizzle in enough water mixture just until dough comes together. Turn out dough onto lightly floured surface; press into a ball. Divide dough in half. Shape each half into a disc; wrap in plastic wrap. Refrigerate 30 minutes.

3. Preheat oven to 425°F. Roll out one pastry disc into 11-inch circle on floured surface. Line 9-inch pie plate with pastry.

4. Combine remaining 1½ cups sugar, cornstarch, tapioca, lemon peel and allspice in large bowl. Add rhubarb and strawberries; toss to coat. Pour into crust.

5. Roll out remaining pastry disc into 10-inch circle. Cut out letters with small cookie cutters, if desired. Seal and flute edge. Brush pastry with beaten egg. Make loop with dough scrap, if desired; place on baking sheet.

6. Bake pie 50 minutes or until pastry is golden brown and filling is thick and bubbly, adding dough loop to oven during last 10 minutes. Cool on wire rack. Serve warm or at room temperature.

*Pie may be covered loosely with foil during last 30 minutes of baking to prevent overbrowning, if necessary.

Makes 8 servings

Raspberry Clafouti

3 **eggs**

⅓ **cup sugar**

1 **cup half-and-half**

2 **tablespoons butter, melted and slightly cooled**

½ **teaspoon vanilla**

⅔ **cup almond flour**

Pinch salt

2 **containers (6 ounces each) fresh raspberries**

1. Preheat oven to 325°F. Generously grease 9-inch ceramic tart pan or pie plate.

2. Attach wire whip to stand mixer. Whip eggs and sugar in mixer bowl on medium speed 4 minutes or until slightly thickened. Add half-and-half, butter and vanilla; mix until well blended. Gradually add in almond flour and salt on low speed. Pour enough batter into prepared pan to just cover bottom. Bake 10 minutes or until set.

3. Remove pan from oven. Scatter raspberries evenly over baked batter. Stir in remaining batter and pour over raspberries.

4. Bake 40 to 45 minutes or until center is set and top is golden. Cool completely on wire rack. Refrigerate leftovers.

Makes 8 to 10 servings

Note: Clafouti (also spelled clafoutis) is a rustic French dish that is made by topping fresh fruit with a custard-like batter and baking. The most famous and traditional clafouti is made with cherries, but berries, plums, peaches and pears can also be used.

Strawberry Heart Cupcakes

1 cup coarsely chopped strawberries, divided

1½ cups all-purpose flour

1 teaspoon baking powder

½ teaspoon baking soda

½ teaspoon salt

¾ cup granulated sugar

1 cup (2 sticks) butter, softened, divided

2 eggs

1 teaspoon vanilla

⅓ cup buttermilk*

4 ounces cream cheese, softened

2 to 2½ cups powdered sugar

6 small strawberries, halved

*Or substitute 1 teaspoon vinegar or lemon juice plus enough milk to equal ⅓ cup. Let stand 5 minutes.

1. Preheat oven to 350°F. Line 12 standard (2½-inch) muffin cups with paper baking cups.

2. Place ¾ cup chopped strawberries in food processor; process until smooth. Reserve 2 tablespoons strawberry puree for frosting.

3. Combine flour, baking powder, baking soda and salt in medium bowl.

4. Attach flat beater to stand mixer. Beat granulated sugar and ½ cup butter in mixer bowl on medium speed until creamy. Add ½ cup strawberry puree until blended. Add eggs and vanilla; beat well. Add flour mixture alternately with buttermilk, beating on low speed just until combined after each addition. Stir in remaining ¼ cup chopped strawberries. Spoon batter evenly into prepared muffin cups.

5. Bake 20 to 22 minutes or until toothpick inserted into centers comes out clean. Cool cupcakes in pan 5 minutes. Remove from pan; cool completely.

6. For frosting, attach flat beater to stand mixer. Beat remaining ½ cup butter, cream cheese and reserved 2 tablespoons strawberry puree in mixer bowl on medium speed until well blended. Gradually add powdered sugar; beat until desired consistency is reached.

7. Fit piping bag with large round tip; fill with frosting. Pipe frosting in swirls on cupcakes. Cut strawberry halves to resemble hearts; top each cupcake with strawberry heart.

Makes 12 cupcakes

Linzer Sandwich Cookies

1⅔ cups all-purpose flour

¼ teaspoon baking powder

¼ teaspoon salt

¾ cup granulated sugar

½ cup (1 stick) butter, softened

1 egg

1 teaspoon vanilla

Powdered sugar (optional)

Seedless red raspberry jam

1. Combine flour, baking powder and salt in medium bowl.

2. Attach flat beater to stand mixer. Beat granulated sugar and butter in mixer bowl on medium speed until light and fluffy. Beat in egg and vanilla until blended. Gradually add flour mixture, beating on low speed until dough forms. Divide dough in half. Wrap each half in plastic wrap; refrigerate 2 hours or until firm.

3. Preheat oven to 375°F. Roll out half of dough on lightly floured surface to ³⁄₁₆-inch thickness. Cut out circles with 1½-inch floured scalloped or plain round cookie cutters. (If dough becomes too soft, refrigerate several minutes before continuing.) Place cutouts 2 inches apart on ungreased cookie sheets.

4. Roll out remaining half of dough and cut out circles. Cut shapes from circles using small cookie cutters. Place 2 inches apart on ungreased cookie sheets.

5. Bake 7 to 9 minutes or until edges are lightly browned. Cool cookies on cookie sheets 2 minutes. Remove to wire racks; cool completely.

6. Sprinkle powdered sugar over cookies with holes. Spread jam on flat sides of whole cookies; top with sugar-dusted cookies. Store tightly covered at room temperature or freeze up to 3 months.

Makes about 2 dozen sandwich cookies

Chocolate Soufflés for Two

1 tablespoon butter plus additional for greasing

2 tablespoons plus 1 teaspoon sugar, divided

4 ounces bittersweet chocolate, broken into pieces

2 eggs, separated, at room temperature

Pinch cream of tartar

1. Preheat oven to 375°F. Coat two 6-ounce soufflé dishes or ramekins with butter. Add ½ teaspoon sugar to dishes; shake to coat bottoms and sides.

2. Combine chocolate and 1 tablespoon butter in top of double boiler. Heat over simmering water until chocolate is melted and smooth, stirring occasionally. Remove from heat; stir in egg yolks one at a time. (Mixture may become grainy, but will smooth out with addition of egg whites.)

3. Attach wire whip to stand mixer. Whip egg whites and cream of tartar in mixer bowl on high speed until soft peaks form. Gradually add remaining 2 tablespoons sugar, beating until stiff peaks form and mixture is glossy. Gently fold egg whites into chocolate mixture, allowing some white streaks to remain. *Do not overmix.* Divide batter evenly between dishes.

4. Bake 15 minutes until soufflés rise but remain moist in centers. Serve immediately.

Makes 2 soufflés

Double Chocolate Pound Cake

3 cups all-purpose flour

2 cups granulated sugar

½ cup unsweetened Dutch process cocoa powder

3 teaspoons baking powder

½ teaspoon salt

1 cup (2 sticks) plus 3 tablespoons butter, softened, divided

1¼ cups milk

1¾ teaspoons vanilla, divided

5 eggs

2 ounces unsweetened chocolate

1 cup powdered sugar

2 tablespoons hot water

1. Preheat oven to 325°F. Grease and flour 12-cup bundt pan.

2. Attach flat beater to stand mixer. Combine flour, granulated sugar, cocoa, baking powder and salt in mixer bowl. Add 1 cup butter, milk, and 1 teaspoon vanilla; mix on low speed 1 minute. Increase speed to medium; beat 2 minutes. Add eggs, one at a time, beating well on low speed after each addition. Beat on medium speed 30 seconds. Pour batter into prepared pan.

3. Bake about 1 hour or until toothpick inserted near center comes out clean. Cool completely in pan on wire rack. Invert onto serving plate.

4. For glaze, melt chocolate and remaining 3 tablespoons butter in small heavy saucepan over low heat, stirring constantly. Stir in powdered sugar and remaining ¾ teaspoon vanilla. Stir in hot water, 1 teaspoon at a time, until glaze reaches desired consistency. Drizzle over cake.

Makes 16 servings.

Chocolate Strawberry Cream Cake

2 cups plus 3 tablespoons sugar, divided

2 cups all-purpose flour

½ cup unsweetened cocoa powder

2 teaspoons baking soda

½ teaspoon salt

1 cup warm water

½ cup (1 stick) butter, melted

½ cup vegetable oil

½ cup buttermilk

2 eggs, at room temperature

3 teaspoons vanilla, divided

1½ cups plus 3 tablespoons heavy cream, divided

1 cup semisweet chocolate chips

½ cup strawberry jam

3 tablespoons sour cream

Fresh strawberries (optional)

1. Preheat oven to 350°F. Grease two 9-inch round cake pans. Line bottoms of pans with waxed paper or parchment paper; grease paper.

2. Attach flat beater to stand mixer. Whisk 2 cups sugar, flour, cocoa, baking soda and salt in mixer bowl.

3. Combine water, butter, oil, buttermilk, eggs and 2 teaspoons vanilla in large bowl; add to flour mixture. Beat on low speed 2 minutes. Pour batter into prepared pans.

4. Bake 35 to 40 minutes or until toothpick inserted into centers comes out clean. Cool in pans 15 minutes. Remove to wire racks; cool completely. Peel off paper.

5. Meanwhile, place 3 tablespoons cream and chocolate chips in small microwavable bowl; microwave on HIGH 40 seconds. Stir until smooth. Cool to spreading consistency.

6. Place one cake layer on serving plate; spread with jam. Spread cooled chocolate mixture over jam. Top with remaining cake layer. Cover loosely; refrigerate 2 hours or up to 2 days.

7. Attach wire whip to stand mixer. Whip remaining 1½ cups cream, 3 tablespoons sugar, 1 teaspoon vanilla and sour cream in mixer bowl on medium-high speed just until stiff peaks form. *Do not overbeat.*

8. Frost top and side of cake with frosting. Refrigerate cake until ready to serve, up to 8 hours. Garnish with strawberries.

Makes 12 servings

Metric Conversion Chart

VOLUME MEASUREMENTS (dry)

⅛ teaspoon = 0.5 mL
¼ teaspoon = 1 mL
½ teaspoon = 2 mL
¾ teaspoon = 4 mL
1 teaspoon = 5 mL
1 tablespoon = 15 mL
2 tablespoons = 30 mL
¼ cup = 60 mL
⅓ cup = 75 mL
½ cup = 125 mL
⅔ cup = 150 mL
¾ cup = 175 mL
1 cup = 250 mL
2 cups = 1 pint = 500 mL
3 cups = 750 mL
4 cups = 1 quart = 1 L

VOLUME MEASUREMENTS (fluid)

1 fluid ounce (2 tablespoons) = 30 mL
4 fluid ounces (½ cup) = 125 mL
8 fluid ounces (1 cup) = 250 mL
12 fluid ounces (1½ cups) = 375 mL
16 fluid ounces (2 cups) = 500 mL

WEIGHTS (mass)

½ ounce = 15 g
1 ounce = 30 g
3 ounces = 90 g
4 ounces = 120 g
8 ounces = 225 g
10 ounces = 285 g
12 ounces = 360 g
16 ounces = 1 pound = 450 g

DIMENSIONS

1/16 inch = 2 mm
⅛ inch = 3 mm
¼ inch = 6 mm
½ inch = 1.5 cm
¾ inch = 2 cm
1 inch = 2.5 cm

OVEN TEMPERATURES

250°F = 120°C
275°F = 140°C
300°F = 150°C
325°F = 160°C
350°F = 180°C
375°F = 190°C
400°F = 200°C
425°F = 220°C
450°F = 230°C

BAKING PAN SIZES

Utensil	Size in Inches/Quarts	Metric Volume	Size in Centimeters
Baking or Cake Pan (square or rectangular)	8×8×2	2 L	20×20×5
	9×9×2	2.5 L	23×23×5
	12×8×2	3 L	30×20×5
	13×9×2	3.5 L	33×23×5
Loaf Pan	8×4×3	1.5 L	20×10×7
	9×5×3	2 L	23×13×7
Round Layer Cake Pan	8×1½	1.2 L	20×4
	9×1½	1.5 L	23×4
Pie Plate	8×1¼	750 mL	20×3
	9×1¼	1 L	23×3
Baking Dish or Casserole	1 quart	1 L	—
	1½ quarts	1.5 L	—
	2 quarts	2 L	—